P9-DHS-841

The Love
Every Woman Needs

The Love Every Woman Needs

Intimacy with Jesus

Jan McCray

Chosen Books

A Division of Baker Book House Co
Grand Rapids, Michigan 49516

© 1997 by Jan McCray

Published by Chosen Books
a division of Baker Book House Company
P.O. Box 6287, Grand Rapids, MI 49516-6287

Third printing, April 1997

Printed in the United States of America

All rights reserved. No part of this publication may be reproduced, stored in a
retrieval system or transmitted in any form or by any means—for example, elec-
tronic, photocopy, recording—without the prior written permission of the pub-
lisher. The only exception is brief quotations in printed reviews.

Library of Congress Cataloging-in-Publication Data

McCray, Jan, 1935–
   The love every woman needs : intimacy with Jesus / Jan McCray.
      p.   cm.
   ISBN 0-8007-9253-X (paper)
      1. Christian women—Religious life. 2. Love—Religious aspects—
Christianity. I. Title.
BV4527.M38   1997
248.8'43—dc21   97-13496

Unless otherwise noted, Scripture quotations are taken from the NEW AMERICAN
STANDARD BIBLE ®, Copyright © The Lockman Foundation 1960, 1962, 1963,
1968, 1971, 1972, 1973, 1975, 1977, 1995. Used by permission.

Scripture marked TM is taken from THE MESSAGE. Copyright © by Eugene H.
Peterson 1993, 1994, 1995. Used by permission of NavPress Publishing Group.

Scripture marked KJV is taken from the King James Version of the Bible.

For current information about all releases from Baker Book House, visit our web site:
http://www.bakerbooks.com

Contents

Acknowledgments

This book is dedicated to all the women who are persisting in making Jesus the Love they need most. In sharing their stories with me, they have enriched my life immensely and helped me in my own journey with the Lover of my soul.

It is also dedicated to my husband, Dave, my best encourager and prayer supporter. He is a daily help in my walk of faith, and I could not do what I do without him.

I also want to thank Christine Willett Greenwald for her invaluable editorial expertise in making this book a reality.

Introduction

This book is about intimacy with Jesus Christ on a level few women have experienced. It was born out of the need I have seen in women to receive the full, unconditional love and acceptance of someone significant. We long for that someone to know us completely, cherish us wholly and touch the deepest needs of our souls. We want a relationship with someone that reaches deep into the recesses of our beings and fulfills us completely.

This need becomes more than a casual desire as our lives move along. It turns into a yearning, gnawing reality that demands satisfaction. If the need is frustrated, we will try (consciously or unconsciously) to fill the hole its absence leaves in our spirits through relationships, performance, denial or even Christian busyness.

Ultimately only Jesus can quiet our raging need for unconditional love and acceptance. Jesus must become more to us than just the Savior we know we need. We must come as well to know Him in the intimacy He offers us.

I hope this book will lead you to a freeing, healing intimacy with Jesus. It weaves together stories of biblical and modern-day women who have struggled to attain such a relationship with Him. Our great Savior died so that our sins might be forgiven and we might enter a oneness with Him that is more than we ever dared to dream.

He truly is the Love every woman needs!

Jan McCray
St. Petersburg, Florida

PART 1

MAKING THE LOVE CONNECTION

1

Putting Your Worst Foot Forward

1 remember the first time I saw Anna. She was hanging up clothes behind the small mission house where I was staying in Kenya, Africa, while I offered short-term service among the most primitive of that country's forty-plus tribes, the Maasai. Anna lived in a nearby village and came once a week to help with the mission laundry. As I watched out the window, I noticed that Anna's eyes sparkled and her face was beautiful. As she worked, she sang the same song over and over, the melody dancing infectiously from her tongue.

Something about her magnetic countenance intrigued me. *What,* I wondered, *does her song mean? I want to know this woman!*

The day was breezy and cooler than usual. As I looked through the window, Anna stopped working for a moment to rub her arms together and shake off some of the chill. She was wearing a colorful *shuka,* the traditional cultural dress for Maasai women. But the thin piece of material wrapped around her body like a giant scarf was not enough protection from the cool weather. So I grabbed a sweater I had brought from home and ran outside to put it on Anna.

She hugged it close.

"Ashay," she said, smiling at me with those dark, shining eyes. *"Ashay."* She took my hand and squeezed it, and together we finished hanging up the wash.

Anna and I became friends, and I began to search for the secret of this woman's serenity and apparent happiness despite a life that was difficult by any standard. She was the mother of six children and the hardest worker I had ever seen.

The Maasai are normally not farmers but warriors and herdsmen. Anna had learned, however, that people who plant crops are able to feed their children, so singlehandedly she had planted an enormous corn crop. She had even dug her own irrigation ditch to catch water during the rainy season. She stored the corn in the family's mud hut, and it became not only their main source of food, but a means of sharing with others in times of drought. Anna never seemed to get tired—and she was always singing that song!

Was Anna a Christian? Yes, she had come to know Jesus as her personal Savior several years before. The faithful work of missionaries in her area had yielded a small community of believers, and the rustic church there often bustled with Maasai who walked many miles to attend services. They would meet for hours, singing and delighting in the testimonies of fellow believers, some of whom had been ostracized from their villages for believing in Christ.

Though Anna took part consistently in church activities and was raising her children in this fellowship of faith, her heart longed for her husband to open his spirit to Jesus. She wanted him to know the peace and gladness she enjoyed. But not only did Anna's husband refuse to believe in Jesus; he persecuted Anna for her faith. He resorted to violence to show his disapproval, sometimes beating her when she returned to her village from worship. Even when she was pregnant with their last child, she came to church bearing bruises and welts. When I asked her about this, she told me, "I cannot stay away from others who love my Jesus! I must sing and pray and listen to the Word. The bruises always go away."

So it was that Anna seemed able to live above fear, in a place where the hardships in her life could not follow. But how?

Could it be her culture? I asked myself. *Maybe people with limited education live less complicated lives than those of us reared in Western societies. Or maybe Anna isn't as introspective as we are and just takes life at face value.*

But I knew deep down that I could not explain away Anna's radiance by mere sociological or psychological factors. Somehow, in some way, I knew Anna had allowed Jesus to touch and heal what I call her aching place.

The Aching Place

Before I could grasp Anna's secret or learn the meaning of her song, I came to realize an important truth, which I observe as I speak to groups of women and counsel my sisters in all walks of life. Here it is: Every woman—single or married, African or African-American, Caucasian, Latino, Asian or Native American—has an aching place that needs to be touched, soothed, healed, restored and regularly filled and refilled throughout the course of her life. Women cannot always explain the source of this deep inner longing. In fact, they may live for years, in relationships or alone, aware of an empty hurt but unable to identify it.

What is the aching place? Like all aches, physical, mental or emotional, it is in some ways indefinable and vague. If we synthesized feminine observations from all over the world, in all the shades of meaning gathered from thousands of human dialects and languages, we *might* be able to describe it.

Failing that, let me offer this definition: The aching place is made up of a woman's deep yearning for forgiveness and acceptance, tenderness and cherishing, genuine caring and unconditional love from some desired person. The aching place in every woman produces longings for affirmation, self-esteem, security and a sense of significance.

Whew! These yearnings touch every aspect of a woman's life, don't they? And this is precisely why the unhealed, unsoothed, unfilled aching place is a raging, throbbing, nagging sore that is not easily subdued and seldom completely satisfied. It can be quieted at certain times but not at others. And when its yearnings reach a boiling point, they may spill over in a cry for help or in what society considers inappropriate behavior. A woman's aching place affects the way she relates to herself, her life circumstances, the individuals in her life—in short, her world.

Do men have an aching place? Since they are human, with God-breathed spirits of their own, the answer is yes. Are their yearnings the same as ours? I could attempt an answer, but I am a woman and will leave that discussion to a man.

Where is a woman's aching place? In her intellect? In the part of her brain that controls her emotions? Is it a function of her hormonal or nervous system and subject, therefore, to the dictates of her bodily health?

As we will discuss in more detail later, women the world over, regardless of culture, generally seek the fulfillment of the deep yearnings of the aching place through emotional or psychological outlets—that is, through relationships, usually with men: fathers, brothers, friends, lovers, husbands. But as each of us knows from experience, relationships, whether with men or with women, inevitably fall short of fulfilling the deepest needs of our hearts. Why? Because relationships are built on the responses of humans to one another, and, since all humans are needy in their own right, human responses can be devastatingly unsatisfactory.

We human beings minister to one another's bodies, minds and emotions with varying degrees of effectiveness. But the aching place is found in a woman's *spirit,* that part of us designed to communicate with God. Jesus explains,

> "When you look at a baby, it's just that: a body you can look at and touch. But *the person who takes shape within* is formed by something you can't see and touch—the Spirit [of God]—and becomes a living spirit."
>
> John 3:6, TM (italics mine)

It follows, then, that God, and only God, can reach down deep enough to touch the aching place in the spirit He created. How does He do it?

The Love Connection

The only way God can touch and heal the aching place in your heart and mine, I believe, is for us to reach out, reach up and make a love connection with Jesus Christ. And the first step in making that connection—there are other steps, which we will explore later in this chapter and in subsequent chapters—is to put our worst foot forward.

"Wait!" you say. "When you want to make a love connection with someone, you put your best foot forward, not your worst."

That certainly sounds more logical. And it seems to be the way many people try to get God's attention—by showing Him how good they are. But in order to begin making a love connection with Jesus, the Love each of us needs most, we need to put our worst foot forward, to admit honestly how sinful we are and how desperately we need Him.

Why do I use the phrase *love connection?* Because God made the first move toward us nearly two thousand years ago when He sent His Son, Jesus, into this world to model

His love by dying for us and rising again. Now the ball is in our court; completing the love connection is up to us.

Anna knew that. The answer to her uniqueness, deep joy and contentment lay, I finally decided, in the *quality* of her relationship with Jesus. Anna had come to live with Jesus in a love connection that is available to us all, but rarely activated.

In Luke 7 we read of another woman who began the love connection. To this day she remains unnamed; the Gospel writer called her "a woman in the city who was a sinner" (verse 37). Yet what happened to her and how she responded is profoundly important for us to understand if we, too, are to make the love connection to Jesus.

Evidently Jesus had been preaching in her area and she heard Him, or heard a lot about Him. She must have been overwhelmed, for He was not only preaching about the Kingdom of God, as did many traveling teachers, but offering forgiveness—and love! It was probably the first time she had ever dared think that the God of Abraham, Isaac and Jacob could actually love her. Could it be true? Oh, how desperately she needed this unconditional love!

And Jesus was different. This woman must have seen incredible tenderness in His eyes as He spoke to the crowds. The love He offered freely seemed like no other. And so, quietly, deep down inside, she took it freely.

It must have been the most rapturous moment of her life, and she went home exploding with love and gratitude, amazed by the change that God's redeeming, accepting love could make in the way she felt about herself, about others and about her future.

Then an opportunity arose to respond to Jesus.

When she learned that He was reclining at table in the Pharisee's house, she brought an alabaster vial of perfume.

Luke 7:37

Jesus had been invited for dinner at the home of Simon, a Pharisee, a religious leader in the community, and this woman felt compelled to see Him. She dared to crash the party!

Actually, it was not as hard back then as we might think to go to a dinner uninvited. The homes were open in design, and dinner was usually served in the garden, where it was cool. Townspeople could stand on the fringes and witness the great social occasions, and often the poor did just that, coming to watch the more affluent in their community eat!

But this woman had no desire to be a simple spectator. She wanted to pour on Jesus the adoration of her heart. He had touched her aching place, offering her hope, forgiveness and acceptance, and filling her with love such as she had never known. She had been a receiver, and now the powerful tide of love in her heart demanded that she be a giver.

What about us? There is a time to hear the claims of Jesus, and there is a time to respond. Often we spend our lives listening but never responding at a heart level, with all of our bodies, minds, emotions and wills.

Some of us who have been raised in the Church have built-in problems with response. We have often heard the message and sung the songs of Jesus. We have received little doses of God Sunday after Sunday, prayer meeting after prayer meeting, until they are like an injection for a disease: The little doses make us immune! Although we respond to Jesus with our minds and intellects, we are so numb that we fail to offer Him the passion of our hearts.

But this woman had no "churchy" background. The Bible says she was a sinner—a term that was always applied to those of immoral character. Most likely she was a prostitute, a woman of the night. The only religion she knew was what she had seen and heard from the spiritual leaders of her day. Some of them may even have been her customers. But we know for certain that she was treated with contempt by the very people who claimed to know God. Listen to the internal comment of Simon, the dinner host, about her:

> "If this man were a prophet He would know *who and what sort of person* this woman is who is touching Him, that she is a sinner."
>
> Luke 7:39 (italics mine)

"Who and what sort of person!" Can't you just hear the disdain in Simon's attitude?

We can only imagine what this woman's life was like, but surely it was one of loneliness, shame, self-loathing and dis-illusionment, having been used by men and rejected by those who paraded their own respectability. The contempt of Simon's dinner guests would be nothing new. All that mattered to her now was getting close to Jesus regardless of the cost. He was the One who had looked at her differently from any other man. He saw beyond her sin and loved her. He did not condone her lifestyle; He forgave it.

So she seized the moment and went to that open court-yard carrying costly oils and perfume to do the only thing she knew to do. She stood at the feet of the Lord Jesus as He reclined on a couch for dinner and,

> weeping, she began to wet His feet with her tears, and kept wiping them with the hair of her head, and kissing His feet, and anointing them with the perfume.
>
> verse 38

Perhaps she looked up into His eyes. Perhaps, aware of the scene she was precipitating, she hid her face as the fra-grance of her oils and perfumes permeated the garden with the aroma of her unabashed love.

Even as she acted, she must have wondered: Would she embarrass Him? Would the love she had seen earlier still be there? Would He understand the gift she was bringing? Would He know that by being there, she was openly admitting her need of Him and her acceptance of His love and future right to be master of her life?

All her fears must have melted away and her doubts turned to faith as she saw the mercy and compassion with which He received her. He did not act embarrassed but accepted her gift graciously. And—wonder of wonders!— when Simon's accusing thoughts and strong disapproval filled the garden, Jesus perceived it and defended her. He said to His host:

> "Simon, I have something to say to you. . . . A certain moneylender had two debtors: one owed five hundred denarii, and the other fifty. When they were unable to repay, he graciously forgave them both. Which of them therefore will love him more?" Simon answered and said, "I suppose the one whom he forgave more."
> And He said to him, "You have judged correctly." And turning toward the woman, He said to Simon, "Do you see this woman? I entered your house; you gave Me no water for My feet, but she has wet My feet with her tears, and wiped them with her hair. You gave Me no kiss; but she, since the time I came in, has not ceased to kiss My feet. You did not anoint My head with oil, but she anointed My feet with perfume. For this reason I say to you, her sins, which are many, have been forgiven, for she loved much; but he who is forgiven little, loves little."
>
> Luke 7:40–46

Yes, the love was still there. Jesus let Simon and his guests know, kindly but firmly, that this woman had done more to minister to Him than all their socially correct, proper hospitality had accomplished. A nameless outcast, one of the dregs of society, had dared to bare her hurting, sinful heart to Jesus. She had put her worst foot forward—and found out that He loved her just the same. That day she began a love connection with Jesus.

Have you?

"How Do I Put My Worst Foot Forward?"

Perhaps you have never understood and accepted the fact that Jesus Christ came to earth as the embodiment of God Himself, and that He offered His life on the cross at Calvary to atone for your sins and mine—to wipe them off the slate of history. Perhaps you have never grasped the amazing reality of His resurrection from the grave, which offers to all who receive His sacrificial gift the promise of eternal life after death. Or perhaps you have known and accepted the Gospel message intellectually but have never let its implications soothe your aching place.

Too many of us find religion but never experience the life change that comes from letting Jesus cleanse everything—from the blackest dirt to the tiniest cobwebs—out of the corners of our lives. We may believe in Jesus and understand enough biblical truth about His life and death to align ourselves with His children. We may be content to know Him from a distance. We work hard and follow the rules. We consider ourselves good people. Yet we never respond to the cleansing, freeing love He offers with unfettered love of our own.

Jesus longs for our love response, because only as we offer it can He begin to touch and heal our aching place. But we can offer that unrestrained love response only when, like Anna and the nameless prostitute, we recognize our own desperately sinful condition and make ourselves vulnerable to the only One who can satisfy our need. This is the first step in making the love connection.

I received a phone call some time ago from a young woman whose husband was a well-known spiritual leader in our town. I had known this family for about five years and marveled at how much time the husband spent outside their home, devoted to his work, his denomination and to local and state civic affairs. It seemed like a lot to juggle.

His wife, the mother of a teenage son and a new baby girl, was petite, vivacious and always looked like a fashion plate. She was easy to like, with a wonderful laugh and conversational skills that made those around her feel comfortable. She had trusted in Christ as Savior at age ten and had, in her words, "walked a straight line" since then. Other women considered her life, family and activities in the local church a model to follow.

But when she called, I could tell by her trembling voice that something was wrong. She asked if I would come to her house so she could talk with me. I went.

At first we made small talk, and I got to hold her adorable baby girl. But when I asked the reason for her call, she began to cry, telling me that her husband's frequent absences had left her feeling neglected, despite the fact that she considered him a fine man and a good father. In fact, she told me, her loneliness had led to an emotional attachment with a married man at church. The situation was tearing her apart inside.

Over and over she defended herself pitiably, saying there had never been anything physical between them. But it was clear that the gnawing inside her was increasing every day. She was miserable, knowing that the relationship was wrong and must stop. She felt guilty and confused, a traitor to her husband and children.

But suddenly she dried her tears and exclaimed, "Jan, I don't understand how this could have happened! I'm always the one at my church helping other people to Christ—I mean, people who really sin and don't lead good lives. How could I have done some of the same things those people do?"

Inwardly I found myself sighing. What she had just said was very revealing. It told me that the gnawing she felt was much more than guilt over the emotional adultery. This young woman had never really thought of herself as a sinner!

"But," you say, "she had made a commitment to Christ at an early age." Yes, but she had never really considered herself a fallen person. She had read her Bible, attended church, served in her community and done "the right things." But she had never understood the depth of what Jesus had done for her—for *her!*—when He died on the cross. Those other people who came to Him were sinners; she was different.

Now she was awakened spiritually, sensing that something deep inside her was kin to those folks she had called sinners. It blew her away, and she had come crashing off the pedestal she had erected for herself. She had always thought Jesus was lucky to have her on His team. Now, faced with the truth about herself, she began once again to cry.

I took her in my arms and rocked her, telling her about the great mercy and love that are ours in Jesus Christ, as if she had never heard these things before.

"He has always known your heart," I said gently. "He has always seen your potential to do this thing. That's why He came to die for you."

"I'm sorry, Jesus!" she cried out.

"He knows, He knows," I said, "and you are forgiven."

That very day, that very hour, my young friend began her love connection with Jesus.

Establishing Your Love Connection

In order to make your own love connection with Jesus, realize your potential for sin. Remember what Jesus has done for you out of the wonderfully tender, self-sacrificing love He showed for you on the cross. Just as real love (not infatuation) between a man and woman begins most often when one recognizes some winning quality of the other's personality, or feels amazed and thankful for some unselfish, kind, tender thing the other has done, so we need to recognize the huge, utterly selfless abundance of love Jesus has placed at our feet, despite our unworthiness.

It is easy, especially if we have grown up in the Church or even gone to church for a long time, to lose sight of the debt of gratitude we owe Jesus. But there is something about real gratitude, gut-level gratitude, that builds intimacy with Him, connects us to His love and enables us to pour out our love to Him in return.

My family experienced that kind of gratitude, intimacy-building and connection to our Lord in a memorable way one year as we celebrated His birthday.

A Christmas Eve Dream

Our three children are all grown now and on their own, but we still like to follow our special family traditions when we get together. One of our favorites is to have a time of singing and Scripture reading before opening our gifts on Christmas morning. Then we take turns going around the circle to give Jesus a thank offering for His blessings. We find it a wonderful way to recognize and honor the day of His birth.

One Christmas morning a few years ago, we were thrilled to have our only grandson, Tyson, his mommy (our daughter) and his daddy with us. Before Tyson's birth we had looked forward to his arrival, but we never knew how much we would love him. When our daughter Shannon and her husband moved from our hometown in Florida to Pennsylvania a year after Tyson was born, it broke our hearts, but we determined to build a relationship with this little one, no matter how far away he lived. In fact, people tell us we ought to buy stock in an airline, we fly to see him so often! But God has honored our commitment to bond with Tyson, and the love has grown.

So on this Christmas morning we went around the circle, each sharing a blessing and giving Jesus the praise of our lips. When we had all spoken, my husband, Dave, asked if he could share a disturbing dream he had had the night before involving Tyson and me. We laughed and told him it must be the pizza he had eaten for our Christmas Eve celebration. But his pensive look told us this was important, so we quieted down to listen.

"In my dream," Dave began, "Mom, Tyson and I were out walking in an unfamiliar place. Thick fog made it hard to see, and the ground was rugged, with steep cliffs nearby. Mom and I were holding Tyson's hands tightly as we made our way through the soup-like density, and we reminded him frequently not to let go. But suddenly Tyson bolted and jumped out ahead of us. We screamed, but neither of us could see or feel him."

Dave's voice began to quiver, and we could see he was reliving the fright of that moment.

"I kept yelling Tyson's name," he continued. "I felt numb, immobile. But before I could think what to do, Mom lunged forward to find him. When she did, we saw that he was right at the edge of an abyss. Mom grabbed Tyson and flung him backwards into my arms, but as she did she lost her footing and was hurled over the edge of the cliff. I stood there holding Tyson and staring down into the dangerous, deep hole. Tyson was safe, but Mom was gone. She had given her life to save him."

By now Dave was weeping softly, and some of us joined him, stunned by the emotion that the dream evoked.

"I know what the dream means," Shannon cried out. "I know why Jesus let Daddy dream that dream the night before Christmas! It's so wonderful—can't you see? We all know how much Mom and Dad love Tyson. Either of them would gladly give their lives to save him, if necessary. They felt protective of him in this dream and wanted to keep him safe in the fog. But when he pulled away and was in danger, Mom immediately jumped out to save him. She never thought about her own safety."

Shannon's voice cracked. "That's why this is so wonderful. Mom did for Tyson what Jesus has done for us. All of us had pulled away from Him; we were separated from Him. We were all in a dangerous place. But His love couldn't bear it. He loved us so much that He lunged to His death to put us in a safe place. That's what Christmas is all about. Jesus came to earth to die so that He could rescue us."

Acknowledging Our Need

I will never forget that Christmas morning when Dave's dream and our daughter's love connection with Jesus helped us picture our Savior rescuing each of us from the abyss. We were indeed in debt because of our sin, and Jesus paid that debt out of His tremendous love. Once we understand our debt, how can we not respond to such love?

The prostitute in Luke 7 understood her debt: She was a sinner and made no excuses. So it was that Jesus observed, "Her sins, which are many, have been forgiven, for she loved much; but he who is forgiven little, loves little" (Luke 7:47).

We may or may not have the prostitute's history of sin. Our sins may appear much less drastic, much more subtle. But a quick check of the Hebrew language offers enlightenment to shake our complacency. The Hebrew—unlike our English, in which the single word *sin* covers many different shades of meaning—offers three words for *sin: transgression,* which means "rebellion"; *iniquity,* with the root of "perverseness" and indicating "mischief"; and *sin,* which signifies "missing the mark" or "to forfeit." (Isaiah 53:5 and 12 offer examples of these three words.)

In essence, *transgression* is the rebellion born in all of us from the fall of Adam and Eve. Transgression is our inborn tendency to turn away from God or think we do not need Him. *Iniquity* is the actual doing of something wrong. And *sin* means to forfeit or simply miss the mark. This can include sins of omission. One sin, in God's eyes, is no worse or better than another; God makes no distinction among sins even though He does say that sexual sin hurts our own bodies and many others. We may have rebelled, committed perverse mischief or simply missed the mark. But, as the old saying goes, "Close counts only in horseshoes." God has a standard of righteousness of which the Bible says all of us—every single human being who ever lived or will live—have fallen short (see Romans 3:23).

Oh, we may acknowledge our sins—theologically, in theory, in our intellects. But we will never be able to love Jesus with the depth and intimacy He wants, and we want, until we put our worst foot forward, approaching Him honestly and openly with grateful hearts, admitting our abysmal need and His overwhelming adequacy to rescue us.

Anna, I came to see, had done this. She not only recognized her great debt and need for a Savior, but she had seen that Jesus' sacrifice had been made out of love for her. Unable to fully comprehend it, she still dared step out and accept it by faith. And so it was that the aching place in the deepest part of her being had been satisfied.

Later I found out the meaning of Anna's song. It was a love song, simple yet profound:

> Hallelujah, hallelujah,
> For the blood of Jesus,
> For the blood of Jesus,
> I sing hallelujah!

Anna knew and acknowledged her need for the blood of Jesus to cleanse her from sin. And she loved Him passionately for doing it!

"I Have Taken the First Step—but It Is Not Enough"

You may know many women, as I do, who have made a commitment to Jesus Christ—establishing a love connection by placing their worst foot forward and accepting His forgiveness—but who still suffer the wrenching pangs of the aching place. You may even be one of them. And right now you may be saying, "I've gladly embraced Him as Savior—as the One who died for my sins, washed me clean through His blood and made eternal life in heaven my future. But I still hurt inside; my aching place constantly cries out for more."

Many women believe they have *completed* the love connection to Jesus by making a profession of faith. But it is possible to accept Jesus as Savior while never connecting to Him in a way that engenders trust and intimacy. We may go to church, pray, attend Bible studies and serve. We may try to live by scriptural principles while never allowing ourselves to be vulnerable enough to Jesus to take the second step: reaching the level of trust it takes to find Him as the Love we need. This kind of trust involves risk, and it frightens us.

I know because I was frightened. In chapters 2 and 3 I will share some of my own journey toward making the love connection with Jesus—a journey that led me to understand from personal experience Anna's inner radiance despite difficult circumstances. I hope that as you read my story, you will find the courage to take the second step in making the love connection. It will free Jesus to do what He longs to do for you: soothe, heal and fill your aching place as only He can.

That soothing, healing and filling will involve a journey for you as well—a journey you and your Love will make together. This book will serve as a guide to some of the places where you may stop and work, process your life experiences, or perhaps just rest and relax on the way to your eternal goal: life with your Love, Jesus Himself, in all His tenderness, love and shining glory.

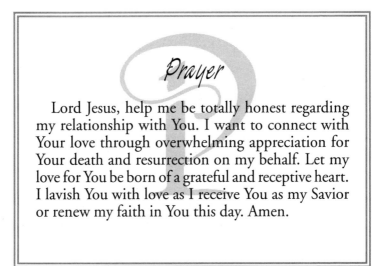

Prayer

Lord Jesus, help me be totally honest regarding my relationship with You. I want to connect with Your love through overwhelming appreciation for Your death and resurrection on my behalf. Let my love for You be born of a grateful and receptive heart. I lavish You with love as I receive You as my Savior or renew my faith in You this day. Amen.

2

Leaping into the Arms of My Love

When our three children were young, Dave and I bought a roomy family home where we lived for almost 25 years. It was not fancy, but it had lots of trees and greenery and offered wonderful stability and lasting memories.

One Saturday we were out raking and bagging leaves. Our purpose was to share a family activity, but Andrew, barely two years old, Shannon, four, and Jana, seven, were there mostly for the companionship and bonding.

Earlier in the day Dave had used a ladder to sweep leaves from our roof so they, too, could be collected. Now Jana was working beside me shoveling leaves into bags, Andrew was playing nearby and I was singing a little song they liked.

Suddenly, in the middle of my song, a tiny voice shouted, "Look at me, Daddy, look at me!"

My heart raced to my throat as I looked up. Shannon had found the ladder still leaning against the house and had climbed to the top of the roof. Standing there in her slippery thongs, our little daughter had no idea of the danger she was in.

What could I do? If I screamed, I might frighten her, possibly causing her to lose her balance. If I scrambled up the ladder to rescue her, it might be too late.

"Dave," I called softly. "Dave."

Then I just stood there, transfixed with fear.

Without a word Dave walked over to the edge of the house.

"Shannon," he said in a normal voice. "Shannon, jump into Daddy's arms." He held his arms open. "Jump into my arms right now, honey."

The next thing I knew, our fragile little girl sailed off that roof into her father's arms, yelling, "Wheeee!" all the way down.

I was shaking all over as I ran to Dave. "Honey, the roof is so high and dangerous. She could have been hurt and—"

Dave stopped me.

"She trusted me, Jan," he said. "She's all right."

By this time Shannon had already wiggled out of Dave's arms and gone off to play with her brother. I did not recover so easily and sank into a nearby lawn chair as the implications of the incident swept over me. Tears flowed as I thanked God for her safety. And I kicked myself for our carelessness in leaving the ladder out to tempt her. But in my innermost spirit, Jesus quieted my anxious heart.

Hush, He seemed to say. *Don't fret, Jan. Just remember, this is the kind of trust I want you to have in Me.*

I sighed. Would I ever trust the Lord that completely?

Long after Shannon's escapade, I thought about what Jesus had whispered in my heart. Why had Shannon jumped from the roof without questioning her dad? She had not hesitated for a moment. Why had she not evaluated the risk? Why had she been so fearless?

Some of the answers to those questions, I realized, lay in her innocence, her extreme youth, her lack of good judgment. But I also realized Shannon had a strong relationship with her father. She had no need to calculate or evaluate. She had heard the voice of someone she loved, someone she knew loved her. She had a connection with this man who was coaxing her to jump, and she never once doubted that he was big enough or strong enough to catch her.

Shannon knew the voice. She trusted the man. She jumped. She made a physical connection with her daddy's arms.

Jesus used Shannon's childish action to show me that she had completed a powerful love connection with her daddy that day. She had demonstrated her love for Dave by trusting him with her very life. And Jesus let me know that I was to trust Him in the same way.

But at that point I was not ready. I wanted to dare to trust my Savior and abandon myself totally to the One who was encouraging me to jump into His arms of love. But I could not. I still had much to learn and plenty of ladders to climb.

The Lover of my life was patient. He continued every day to show me His grace in little but unmistakable ways. He knew—and I knew, deep inside—that one day I would take the leap of total vulnerability and trust, as Shannon had. One day I would complete the love connection.

Looking Back . . .

I had always gone to church. We lived in rural Alabama during my early years, and my mother played the piano for our small Methodist congregation. When I was nine we moved to Florida and got involved in a church there. But it was not until age fourteen that I heard, for the first time, the claims of the Gospel of Jesus Christ.

If it had been explained to me clearly before, it had never registered. This night was different. I listened to the familiar story of God's love and was suddenly overcome with the desire to give my heart to Jesus. He had died for me personally, I realized. And in my mind's eye, I could actually see Him standing, smiling, urging me to come to Him. I went gladly, knowing that in this experience I was becoming a child of God. Heaven, I knew, would someday be my home, and it thrilled my whole being.

Then I began to read the Bible with fervor. I almost inhaled it! And I tried to evangelize everyone around me, often doing more harm than good. I became president of my church youth group and wrote the lessons for our Sunday evening youth meetings because I thought our denominational publications were not strong enough in evangelism. Filled with an intense desire to preach the Gospel and reach the millions in the world who did not know the love of Jesus, I purposed in my heart to become a missionary.

During my college years, however, I realized God was moving me in another direction. I married Dave, had a family and taught school. But I was always active in my local church, teaching Sunday school and leading a women's group.

After some time, I decided I was becoming something of an expert on the Bible.

Enter Gina

About fifteen years into my marriage, Gina came on the scene. She was like no one I had ever known. A young mother who had been divorced and was now remarried, Gina was raising two children from her previous marriage and a third child with her new husband. They came to everything the church offered and were eager to learn and grow.

Gina started attending the women's group I led, always coming with a long list of questions. Never content with the Bible study once I presented it, she pressed for more. She wanted to know how to make Jesus Lord of her life; how to accept His unbelievable love and incorporate it into her everyday life and family problems; how to have Jesus sweep her up in this love she kept hearing about.

I began to dread seeing Gina! She sought gut-level application for everything the Bible taught, and I did not know how to give it to her. I knew the Scriptures and could answer any conceptual questions she posed, but Gina asked about the deep, intimate things of God. She spoke of Jesus with anticipation, and it was hard to miss the hunger and thirst of her soul.

What was I to do? Even though I was well-versed in God's Word and had the Christian life pretty well figured out— or so I thought—I recognized my inadequacy to help Gina. In fact, deep inside, my own spirit was beginning to yearn for more of what she craved. In my pride and snobbishness I had always thought, *I'm saved and going to heaven when I die. Isn't that enough?*

But day by day Gina's obsession became mine. She messed up my tidy spiritual world. She upset my logical, intellectual approach to knowing and sharing Jesus. She radically altered all the things I considered "enough" to being a Christian. Without even knowing it, she ripped off the Band-Aids of respectability and religiosity with which I was covering my partially healed aching place. I was in pain.

Desperately I began to study the life of Jesus Christ and the nature of God. I had many questions and many unsettled feelings. But as I searched God's Word, Jesus began to show me what was missing in my relationship with Him. It seemed to have something to do with the threefold nature of God and, more specifically, with the third Person of the Trinity, the Holy Spirit.

I knew a little about the Holy Spirit. He had helped me believe in Jesus in the first place (see John 6:44; John 15:26), He lived in me as a believer (see Romans 8:9) and He helped me understand the Bible (see John 14:26). And I was grateful for the times He had been my Comforter (see John 14:16–17, KJV).

But Jesus knew, and I learned, that I was not yet experiencing true friendship with this third Person of the Trinity. Jesus also knew I had lots of miseducation and baggage from past experiences that were blocking such a relation-

ship. He had to expose each false concept and replace it
with a right, biblical one.

My journey lasted well over a year. (I will share some
specifics in chapter 3.) I read all I could find and talked to
a few, chosen people I thought I could trust. But I had a
sickening fear deep inside that if I got too close to the truth
about the Holy Spirit, I would become more vulnerable to
God than I wanted to be.

How patient and gentle Jesus was with me during this
time! I had no idea, not an inkling, about how He was going
to satisfy my hunger for Him and start me on the road to
intimacy with Him. Nor did I have a clue that I was about
to complete the love connection with Him that I had started
many years before as a fourteen-year-old girl.

I Make the Leap of Submission

About this time our local Methodist church held a week
of special services. Dave and I attended as a matter of course.

I had not shared with our pastor, even though he was
one of the most loving and godly men I have ever known,
my hunger for more of Jesus or my most recent journey
into the Scriptures. After all, he thought I had it all together,
and he admired my knowledge of God's Word. Why should
I tell him how bewildered I really felt?

One night at the close of the week, our guest leader
gave an invitation: "If anyone here tonight would like to
experience a relationship with the Holy Spirit, please come
forward."

What? I screamed inside. *Did I hear you correctly?*

Never had I heard such an invitation! But while I was
still getting over the shock, the leader went on to invite
those who needed prayer for healing.

"Honey, why don't you go forward and have them pray
for your back?" Dave whispered in my ear.

Well, it was true that for a long time I had suffered from back problems; sometimes they left me bedridden for days. But at that moment my back was the furthest thing from my mind. That man had just said to come forward if I wanted a relationship with the Holy Spirit. What did he mean? What would happen to me?

I had no idea, but I had not been able to escape the feeling that the Holy Spirit had more to offer me than I had received. And I knew enough from my study to realize that what the leader was offering was not a strange new doctrine.

I literally ran toward the altar to receive prayer. And that evening several people prayed for me to receive the Holy Spirit in His fullness.

I heard no bells that night. I saw no flashing lights. But I did feel a deep sense of peace and love. It reminded me of the night I had received Jesus as my Savior. And why not? There is only one God, but in the unity of His marvelous Godhead are three eternal and co-equal Persons, the same in substance but unique and different in function. Why would the Holy Spirit seem strange and foreign to me if I knew the Son and the Father?

I also saw that the indwelling Spirit had caused me to hunger and thirst for more of Jesus. Now I wanted a different, deeper level of relationship with Him. I wanted intimacy. I wanted to trust Him completely.

Back at home later that evening, I drifted off to sleep saying over and over again, *I love You, Jesus. I love You so much!*

The next day I felt a warm sense of the presence of God. I got the children off to school as usual, after which it was part of my normal Christian walk to pray. But I could not wait to pray! And my prayer time on this day was different. As I began to talk to Jesus, it was as if He walked into the room. The reality of His presence flooded my surroundings, and I felt His arms around me as surely as if they had been Dave's or one of our children's.

Then the very Holy Spirit of God whispered into the recesses of my being, *I love you, Jan. I love you, daughter.*

I wept and worshiped Him there that morning. Tears of joy and responsive love, like nothing I had ever experienced, poured down my cheeks. I believed Him. I had known God's love in my head for a long time, but now He was placing it in my spirit.

He loves me, I kept saying to myself. *He really loves me!*

I did not know it then, but I had completed the love connection and could feel a trickle of healing begin to flow through my spirit to my aching place.

Was this experience the cure-all for my aching place? No. Making the love connection was the *beginning* of the healing of my aching place—a process that has continued from that day, nearly 25 years ago, to this.

Aside from salvation, no one revelation or experience in the Christian life is a once-for-all thing, not even an experience with the Holy Spirit. In most of God's dealings with us, He seems to follow the model He set in motion at creation: the model of growth and maturing as a process. *Any* relationship matures progressively over time, through interaction and communication, and that includes a relationship with the Holy Spirit. As each of us submits to our great Lover, we take more and more steps with Him into a deeper relationship and a love so unsearchable that it will take a lifetime and eternity to experience even a fragment of it.

But once you believe in your spirit that Jesus loves you, and that His Holy Spirit can interpret and express His love to you specifically, practically and realistically, you and your Love are on your way. You have made the love connection.

"It Didn't Work for Me"

You may be excited right now, eager to learn more, ready to enter into a love connection with Jesus by putting your worst foot forward to acknowledge your tremendous need for Him. You may be ready to respond to Him, submitting yourself in trust to a deep relationship with Him through the Holy Spirit.

Or you may be thinking, *I've made a profession of faith and heard a hundred sermons on the Holy Spirit. What's the big deal? Why do you think your "love connection" will make any difference in my life, or in my so-called aching place?*

This was the experience of a woman I met. I was running down a long corridor at a women's retreat center when this young woman grabbed my arm.

"Jan," she said, "could I talk with you privately?"

I agreed, and we met a short time later.

"You probably won't remember what we talked about the last time I saw you," she began.

But I did remember, even though much time had elapsed since I had seen her.

"We talked about the Holy Spirit, didn't we?" I said.

"That's right," she said. "But I want you to know it didn't work for me. I did exactly what everyone said to do, but nothing changed."

Have you or someone you know gone through a similarly disappointing and depressing experience? You received Jesus as Savior, began to attend church and perhaps joined a Bible study or some other spiritual growth group. As time went along, you kept hearing about a "deeper walk" with Jesus, and that more was available spiritually than what you seemed to have. You heard stories of other women's experiences—stories like mine. And the women with those wonderful stories appeared to have their spiritual lives all figured out. They seemed to be on intimate terms with Jesus.

So you decided to test the spiritual waters. You said the prayer that "worked" for someone else, or you began a new spiritual regimen recommended by a respected Christian leader. You wanted to see if this "Holy Spirit thing" would fill and heal the emptiness, the aching place, inside you.

But what happened to those women with the wonderful stories never happened to you. And you decided that for some reason you failed to qualify for a deeper experience with God. Or maybe, just maybe, this Holy Spirit thing was a lot of emotional gibberish. And your aching place ached more than ever before.

Obstacles to Connecting with the Holy Spirit of Jesus

Jesus, the great Lover of our souls, wants each of us to walk in intimacy and closeness with Him through His Spirit. This intimacy is not some frivolous accessory dreamed up by mystics or off-their-rocker fanatics, but it is part of His plan. Jesus knows that the Holy Spirit, in His fullness, draws us to a place that transcends time and circumstances—a relationship of oneness in which His healing love begins to penetrate our aching place.

But Satan, the archenemy of God, delights to throw obstacles in the way of anyone who hungers for more of Jesus. And Satan has at least four obstacles of choice when it comes to keeping believers from completing the love connection with Jesus through the Holy Spirit:

1. The formula trap;
2. The deception of spiritual greed;
3. Fear of losing control; and
4. Misconceptions about the Holy Spirit.

1. The Formula Trap

Satan is always pleased when he can get our eyes off our relationship with Jesus and onto formulas, methods and programs. He knows that if he entangles us in pursuing the "correct" ways and means to completing the love connection, we will look quickly to the ways and means, and not to Jesus, our Lover.

God's Word offers absolutely no manmade formula, no spiritual regimen, no complicated hoops that you and I must jump through in order to enter a relationship with Him through the Holy Spirit. The only requirement is being reconciled to the Father through His Son, Jesus Christ, who cleanses us from our sin and bridges the great chasm between us and His holiness. Once that requirement has been met, the picture God's Word draws to show us how to make the connection is relational. Listen to Jesus:

> "Suppose one of you fathers is asked by his son for a fish; he will not give him a snake instead of a fish, will he? Or if he is asked for an egg, he will not give him a scorpion, will he? If you then, being evil, know how to give good gifts to your children, how much more shall your heavenly Father give the Holy Spirit to those who ask Him?"
>
> Luke 11:11–13

> "I will ask the Father, and He will give you another Helper, that He may be with you forever; that is the Spirit of truth . . . You know Him because He abides with you, and will be in you."
>
> John 14:16–17

Asking and getting. Giving and receiving. Entering a relationship with the Holy Spirit is as simple as that.

Just as we meet and make friends in a variety of ways and settings, so God draws us into intimate friendship with the Holy Spirit in different ways and settings. Someone you know may have prayed a certain prayer; another may have gone to a special meeting at church (as I did). One woman may connect with the Holy Spirit quietly while she prays alone at home. Another may experience a visible and audible emotional release while praying in a group.

In his classic devotional book *My Utmost for His Highest,* the great Bible teacher Oswald Chambers wrote, "Never make a principle out of your own experience. Let God be as original with others as He is with you." The implication is clear: Both how your love connection with Jesus occurs and how it plays out in your life will be as unique as you are. It is not a formula at all. It is an extension of the relationship we began with Jesus at salvation—a willful choice to enter a deeper union, a more satisfying bond with Jesus through His Spirit.

Never try to follow someone else's path or formula into this relationship. You will always be disappointed.

2. The Deception of Spiritual Greed

I have come to recognize, in the years since Gina first exposed my aching place, that I have never met a person living an unreserved, abandoned, joyful life with Jesus who has not yearned for that kind of relationship with a passion. God honors this hunger in a precious way and promises to fill us up: "Blessed are those who hunger and thirst for righteousness, for they shall be satisfied" (Matthew 5:6).

In fact, whenever we experience a yearning for God so strong that we will do whatever it takes to get closer to Him, we can be sure of one thing: He Himself planted that craving in our spirits. As Jesus said, "No one can come to Me, unless the Father who sent Me draws him. . ." (John 6:44). If you have that kind of longing, be assured that God is already working to fill you in ways you may not realize!

But Satan is amazingly deceitful, and it is all too easy for him to plant in us a greed for God's *gifts* that easily masquerades as genuine spiritual hunger for *God.* Our motive for an alliance with God must always be an acute hunger for Him, not a selfish desire to clutch to ourselves or show

off to the world what He can do for us. Hebr[...]
us that the person "who comes to God must
He is, and that He is a rewarder of those who
Not His gifts. Him.

Completing the love connection with Jesus [...]
Spirit is not something we do to keep up with the joneses,
spiritually speaking. It is not an experience we seek so as to
reassure ourselves that we are not missing out on a spiritual
high others seem to have. If you feel, as my friend did, that
a love relationship with Jesus through the Holy Spirit did
not work for you, try evaluating your motives. Are you
searching for the Giver—or the gifts?

3. Fear of Losing Control

The misguided fear that I would lose control of myself
if I dared to make the love connection with Jesus through
the Holy Spirit was one of the biggest obstacles in my search
for intimacy with my Love.

Part of the reason for this was that, growing up in rural
Alabama, I had been exposed to stories, conjectures and
fears about the reportedly bizarre activities of some Christians known as "holy rollers." I dislike labels and mean no
disrespect by this term. In actuality, I never had a conversation with anyone who understood the Holy Spirit as the
holy rollers did. All I knew was hearsay and rumor.

But as I began my search for a walk with Jesus in the
Holy Spirit, all of those childhood scare stories overtook
me. I had a tremendous anxiety that the closer I got to the
Holy Spirit, the more vulnerable I would become to saying things suddenly that I did not wish to say or doing
things I had no wish to do. I had a nagging suspicion that
the price I would have to pay for unreserved closeness with
Jesus was that, at any minute, I might be thrown into con-
vulsions or foam at the mouth. My prayers during those
days of groping must have sounded like those of a fright-

ened child, asking Jesus to be gentle with me as He jolted me abruptly into the weird and frenzied creature I just *knew* I had to become!

How my delightful Love, Jesus, must have shaken His head in rueful amusement over my groundless apprehensions. For now that I know Him better, I realize that is all they were—groundless apprehensions.

4. Misconceptions about the Holy Spirit

Where do we get some of our strange notions about the Holy Spirit? Some of them come from folks who know little more than we do about the Spirit, or who relate to Him in ways that are confusing or unattractive to us. Others come from people who profess to be filled with God's Spirit but who have made their experience with the Giver (their "formula") more important than the Giver Himself. They seem proud and haughty, perhaps making us feel like second-class citizens in the Body of Christ because we have not had their experience. Militant in their approach about our need for the Holy Spirit, they only end up turning us off.

Of all the strange notions about the Christian faith, the layers of misconception concerning the Holy Spirit are probably the thickest. Many of these come from misunderstanding what God says about the Holy Spirit in His Word, the Bible. But God cannot fill us with His Holy Spirit if we are already full of fears, doubts and misconceptions.

In the early stages of your own hunger for more of Jesus, you may think you know a lot about the Holy Spirit. I thought I did. And you may have much intellectual knowledge about Him. But this head knowledge may not have sifted down to penetrate your spirit.

Or maybe you know very little about the Holy Spirit. You can remedy that by searching God's Word. In the next chapter I want to share with you what I learned about the Holy Spirit during my year of Bible study, before I ran down the aisle at my church to leap into His arms as Shannon leaped into Dave's.

Women of God are wise to gain a biblical perspective about the Holy Spirit, so our love connection with our Lord is built on the solid rock of Scripture.

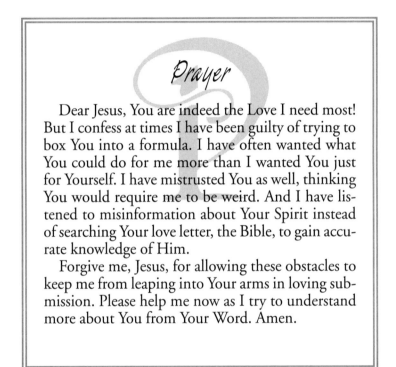

Prayer

Dear Jesus, You are indeed the Love I need most! But I confess at times I have been guilty of trying to box You into a formula. I have often wanted what You could do for me more than I wanted You just for Yourself. I have mistrusted You as well, thinking You would require me to be weird. And I have listened to misinformation about Your Spirit instead of searching Your love letter, the Bible, to gain accurate knowledge of Him.

Forgive me, Jesus, for allowing these obstacles to keep me from leaping into Your arms in loving submission. Please help me now as I try to understand more about You from Your Word. Amen.

3

What the Bible Says about the Holy Spirit

A young woman named Gloria told me once that, shortly after moving with her family to a new city, she found herself feeling anxious and depressed. In fact, it grew hard for her to get out of bed in the morning.

Gloria fought her feelings by herself for a while, then sought out a Christian counselor. She confided to the counselor that she had left a good friend behind in her former hometown and now felt a cloud of sadness hanging over her, hindering her adjustment to her new situation. She and her friend had met at a P.T.A. function and had become jogging mates, sharing heartfelt discussions about their children, their parenting skills and, best of all, their faith in God.

"As I wept out my tale of woe that day in her office," Gloria told me, "she helped guide me back to my own close relationship with Jesus. I began to see Him in my mind's eye—Jesus, my very best Friend, ready to run with me each morning!"

And the next day, as soon as the children left for school, Gloria jogged out to the park, accompanied by the Holy Spirit of Jesus.

"He is here with me as surely as anyone has ever been," she explained. "He listens and speaks and we share many wonderful secrets together."

47

Not long ago, when Gloria's mother died, Gloria's runs with Jesus sustained her.

"He understood my loss in a significant way," she told me, "and I was deeply comforted. I'm getting to know this Friend better and better. He's more than just the Savior of the world. He's my Savior and my Lover. He is real!"

Gloria's story highlights how the presence of the Spirit of Jesus can transform negative circumstances into positive ones and offer comfort, friendship and a listening ear. How do I know Gloria is not making all this up, fabricating a soothing tale to fool me or ease her own pain? Because her experience is grounded in scriptural truth about the presence of Christ in our lives through the Holy Spirit.

Let's consider the biblical answers to three questions in order to understand facts about the Holy Spirit that offer practical, personal help from Jesus for your everyday situation and mine. The questions are:

1. What is the Trinity?
2. What can we expect the Holy Spirit to do in us?
3. What will the Holy Spirit *not* do in us?

1. What Is the Trinity?

While the word *Trinity* is not found in Scripture, the concept is unmistakably there. The doctrine of the Trinity, referring to the three-part nature of God as Father, Son and Holy Spirit, is a set of beliefs that has baffled and astounded theologians (not to mention ordinary Christians) throughout the centuries. Yet it is an integral part of our realization of God as our Love.

For me, understanding the role of each Person of the Trinity was the key to seeing why my love connection with Jesus was incomplete, why the aching place in my spirit still throbbed with pain. Let's look at each Person in turn.

The Father

God the Father, the great and majestic Creator and Ruler of the universe, is ever and everywhere present. "Do I not fill the heavens and the earth?" He asks in Jeremiah 23:24. God the Father is also all-powerful. Jeremiah exclaimed, "Thou hast made the heavens and the earth by Thy great power and by Thine outstretched arm! Nothing is too difficult for Thee" (32:17). And Jesus said emphatically, "With God all things are possible" (Matthew 19:26).

God, who is all-knowing, knew from the beginning of time that men and women, whom He created out of a tremendous longing to share His great love, would wander from a relationship with Him and fall into the terrible separation from Him that we call sin. So He set in motion a plan of salvation for the world that began with a system of blood sacrifice for the atonement of sin. This system, described in the Old Testament (see Leviticus 1–7, 16–17), was always meant to be temporary, a shadow of what was to come.

The Son

God's long-range, eternal plan was to come to earth Himself and be the final sacrifice for our sin, thus opening the door for us to make the love connection with Him. He did exactly that, and came to earth in the Person of Jesus, the Son, who was born of a woman, with blood in His veins! That blood had to be shed if there was to be forgiveness of sin, for the Scriptures clearly state that "without shedding of blood there is no forgiveness" (Hebrews 9:22). And this sacrifice was once for all. In the Old Testament the blood sacrifice had to be repeated over and over. But the work on the cross of God the Son was final and complete.

Thus, it was God the Father who sent the Son into the world, and it was the role of the Son to be the perfect sacrificial Lamb, to lay down His life to atone for our sin and set us free to be in a love relationship with God. Ultimately He was raised from death and returned to His heavenly home.

The Spirit

Now—what about the Holy Spirit? He, too, has always been God. We know that He, like the Father, is all-knowing, for in 1 Corinthians 2:10 we read that "the Spirit searches all things, even the depths of God." Verse 11 tells us that "the thoughts of God no one knows except the Spirit of God." And from Psalm 139:7 we learn that the Holy Spirit is also ever-present: "Where can I go from Thy Spirit?"

The Holy Spirit's role in the Old Testament was different than His role today. Back then He was given to various people to help them carry out certain tasks and services to God. He did not live in believers permanently as He does today. In 1 Samuel 16:13, for example, we find the prophet Samuel taking a horn of oil and anointing young David, a shepherd, as the future king of Israel. "The Spirit of the LORD came mightily upon David from that day forward." God had given David His Holy Spirit for the task of being king.

The Holy Spirit was also given to various prophets so they would have courage to speak God's Word. Second Chronicles 15:1–2 says,

> Now the Spirit of God came on Azariah the son of Oded, and he went out to meet Asa [the king] and said to him, "Listen to me, Asa, and all Judah and Benjamin: the LORD is with you when you are with Him. And if you seek Him, He will let you find Him; but if you forsake Him, He will forsake you."

The Spirit was also given to Gideon, the youngest son of an apparently less-than-influential family from the tribe of Manasseh, so he could effect a tremendous military victory for God's glory (see Judges 6:34–7:25).

It is also clear from the Old Testament that God could not only give the Holy Spirit but withdraw Him. We read in 1 Samuel 16:14 that the Holy Spirit, who had been given to David's predecessor, King Saul, departed from Saul. And you probably recall David's heartfelt prayer, found in Psalm 51, when he repented of an adulterous relationship with Bathsheba. "Do not cast me away from Thy presence," he prayed, "and do not take Thy Holy Spirit from me" (verse 11). David realized the awesomeness of this gift from God, and that the Holy Spirit could be removed from him.

It was at Pentecost, after Jesus had died, been resurrected, appeared to about five hundred believers and then returned to heaven to be with the Father, that the Holy Spirit was given—as Jesus promised He would be—to indwell believers permanently (see Acts 1:8; 2:1–4). We who have been in the Church for years need to sense with renewed wonder the enormity of this gift that is ours as born-again Christians. We are most blessed by the Father to have the joy of His Spirit residing in us the moment we trust Jesus as our personal Savior.

The Mystery

You still may be asking, How can God be Three yet One? Or, as a young Maasai student once put it, "How can Jesus pray to God when He *is* God?"

No analogy of the Trinity can come close to defining this marvelous and infinite mystery, but here is one I learned from an unknown source. It helped my Maasai friend and it has helped me.

Consider the sun. It gives daylight to the whole world, yet it does not have to leave heaven in order for us to enjoy its light. We see sunlight all around us, yet when we look back up into the sky, the sun is still there. The energy of the sun provides warmth and comfort on the earth. Its rays cause the plants and trees to grow, and they give us vitamin D, so vital to our health. Yet the sun never leaves heaven.

The Trinity is similar. God the Father is like the sun—all-powerful, majestic, residing in heaven yet never contained by it.

Jesus is like the light of the sun. The Bible even calls Him the Light, sent to earth to dispel the darkness of our sin (see John 1:8–9; Luke 1:76–79). Jesus Himself said, "I am the light of the world" (John 8:12). He came to show us the Father as He truly is, to illuminate Him to all humankind. But the Father (the sun) did not have to leave heaven in order to send Jesus (the light) to the earth.

The Holy Spirit is like the energy of the sun: He causes growth. God the Father sends His Spirit to live in us when we receive Jesus, offering strength and energizing power so we can grow in Him. And still God the Father, like the sun, remains in heaven reigning over the universe, even though, by His Spirit, He lives in you and me.

God the Father, God the Son and God the Holy Spirit: eternal, coequal Persons with their own distinct personalities and roles. Yet they are One. And in their Oneness, they offer themselves to you and me as the complete, incomparable Love who will never let us go!

2. What Can We Expect the Holy Spirit to Do in Us?

The work of the Holy Spirit is vast, yet few of us realize how this shy member of the Trinity permeates God's work throughout the world and stays within *and* by the side of each individual believer in loving constancy and devotion. Let me explain.

Many people believe the Christian Church was born at Pentecost, but actually it began when Jesus breathed on His disciples and said, "Receive the Holy Spirit" (John 20:22). This birthing was actualized in a profound way at Pentecost because it was then that the Holy Spirit came to indwell believers permanently. God realized the Church could not grow without this enduement. The Holy Spirit brings about the new birth in each believer. None of us could trust Jesus for salvation from sin without the help of the Spirit.

Why is that? Because:

The Holy Spirit convicts us of sin. "And [the Holy Spirit], when He comes, will convict the world concerning sin, and righteousness, and judgment; concerning sin, because they do not believe in Me" (John 16:8–9). Regardless of where we heard the Gospel message or who was preaching or teaching, it was the Spirit Himself who caused us to be aware of our sinful condition.

The Spirit helps us trust Jesus for our salvation. John 6:44 says (as we have seen) that no one comes to Jesus unless the Father draws him. Paul tells us, "Now the Lord *is* the Spirit" (2 Corinthians 3:17, italics mine). And because John 16:13 points out that the Spirit "will not speak on His own initiative," but speaks what the Father tells Him to speak, the Father draws us to Jesus through the Holy Spirit's nudging.

The Spirit brings alive our dead spirits. Sin killed our spirits (see Ephesians 2:1–2, 5), but Jesus told Nicodemus, "Unless one is born of water and the Spirit, he cannot enter into the kingdom of God. That which is born of the flesh is flesh; and that which is born of the Spirit is spirit" (John 3:5–6). So the Spirit "births" us when we trust Jesus.

The Spirit jump-starts us! This happens "by the washing of regeneration and renewing by the Holy Spirit" (Titus 3:5).

And the Holy Spirit does still more! Jesus, speaking first on earth and later through His servant Paul, said that the Spirit would:

Seal us, or put a deposit on us, until our redemption is complete in heaven (see Ephesians 1:13–14).

Help or, in the King James Version, comfort us (see John
   15:26).

Help us to pray as needed (see Romans 8:26).

Teach us (see John 14:26).

Remind us what Jesus said that we need to remember
   (see John 14:26).

Guide us, both generally and specifically (see Romans
   8:14; Acts 8:29).

Help us see the glory of Jesus, so we can become more
   like Him (see 2 Corinthians 3:18).

Restrain, or hold back, evil (see 2 Thessalonians 2:7).

If there is any doubt in your mind, after the above list,
that the Holy Spirit is a Person, let me note that He also

Has feelings (see Ephesians 4:30), which include grief
   or hurt (again, see Ephesians 4:30) and outrage (see
   Hebrews 10:29).

Is intelligent (see 1 Corinthians 2:10–11).

Can be lied to (see Acts 5:3).

Can be resisted (see Acts 7:51).

Above all, the Holy Spirit is a gift from God, as Romans
5:5 declares. He is not a reward for good behavior!

What can we expect, then, from a new closeness to Jesus
in the Holy Spirit? We can expect to see more of Jesus in
our lives. He wants our alliance with Him to be so close
that it is hard to tell where He begins and we end, or where
we begin and He ends. He wants to swoop us up by His
love into affinity and joy with Himself, and then for that
love to overflow into our lives and touch all of our relationships, our circumstances and our world!

We are filled by the Holy Spirit, according to all four
Gospel writers, by an act of our Lover, Jesus. John the Bap-
tist said, "I baptized you with water; but He [Jesus] will

baptize you with the Holy Spirit" (Mark 1:8; see also Matthew 3:11; Luke 3:16; John 1:33).

The Holy Spirit plants the gnawing desire for more of Jesus in our hearts, and Jesus satisfies that desire by baptizing us with His Spirit. We have already received the indwelling of the Spirit at our salvation. His Spirit is within us for the potential of fruit-bearing and power. But in this baptism we experience more yieldedness to His presence and will and deeper fellowship in His company, for He longs for us to enjoy His company. Never let anyone tell you that you do not have the Holy Spirit if you are a born-again Christian. But has Jesus baptized you in His Spirit? You have Him, to be sure, but in this baptism He will have more of you! He wants us to receive all He has for us and become all we can be for Him.

3. What Will the Holy Spirit *Not* Do in Us?

Many Christians think they have "tried" the Holy Spirit or had an experience with Him, but they have become disillusioned and disconnected because they had unbiblical expectations about what the Holy Spirit would do in their lives. We need to examine such expectations carefully and realize these are usually obtained from false assumptions, from misunderstanding the Scriptures and from observing other Christians and their claims.

False Expectation 1: Making the love connection with Jesus through the Holy Spirit is the same as walking in the Spirit. "Walking in the Spirit" is just what it sounds like—deliberately placing one foot in front of the other spiritually as we learn to yield daily to the Savior's love, as we learn to obey the laws of His Kingdom and allow His Spirit to scrutinize our hearts and lives in the loving way only He can do.

Making the love connection with Jesus through the Holy Spirit is a step in the right direction, but it does not guarantee that we will allow the Spirit to rule in our hearts. It does not guarantee that we will set our wills to follow our Lover's will or our feet to follow in His footsteps.

We can never lose the indwelling of the Holy Spirit, praise God, but we can "leak out the filling" if we do not abide, or maintain day-by-day, step-by-step fellowship with Jesus. And that does not happen by magic; it happens by obedience.

False Expectation 2: When I am filled with God's Holy Spirit, I will be a super-Christian, never saying or doing anything wrong. This common misconception about the Holy Spirit's activity in our lives would certainly solve a lot of problems! But it is not true. Being filled with God's Holy Spirit is no magical substitution for regular Bible study, a disciplined prayer life, wholehearted worship and devotion to the Lord or fellowship with other believers. These biblically sound privileges and exercises of our faith are the means God has given us for developing our Christian character, resupplying our "filling" and keeping us close to our Lover.

Every relationship (as I said earlier) is a process, and that includes a relationship with our Love, Jesus, through the Holy Spirit. Our characters are not suddenly perfected, but we continue to become in experience what we immediately became, by grace, the moment we first believed. Colossians 3:10 tells us that our new selves are "being renewed." Second Corinthians 4:16 refers to the inner person "being renewed day by day." The reality of Jesus' love for us, and ours for Him, deepens and grows with each new encounter and daily, nitty-gritty surrender to living Jesus' way through the power of His Spirit. But the Holy Spirit is not offered us as a shortcut in the relational process!

False Expectation 3: Being filled with God's Holy Spirit will make me an instant preacher or evangelist. Being filled with the Holy Spirit, and allowing Him to walk in and live through us daily, will make us become more like our Lover and able, therefore, to access His power for each task He puts in front of us. And, yes, the Holy Spirit can help us overcome our fears and shyness about sharing the Good News of Jesus, if we continue to tune in to Him.

But the Bible is clear about the uniqueness of each believer, in personality and in what spiritual gifts for ministry the Holy Spirit shares with us as we draw closer and closer to Him. That is another subject, and many good books have been written to help you understand it. For the purpose of our discussion, it is important to remember that it is your *relationship* with Jesus, your Love, on which He wants you to focus. When you need special help for special tasks, He will come through.

These, then, are three of the most common false expectations about the Holy Spirit. Depending on your background and experience, you may have more. It is vital to check them against Scripture so your relationship with your Lover through the Spirit is not based on mistaken human ideas.

If you listen to ballads about human love for any length of time, you realize how fickle it is—how precariously balanced on the mistaken notions that human love can accomplish anything or on "warm fuzzies" that fade all too fast in the light of life's realities. Our heavenly Love offers us a different kind of relationship. He is the Lord of reason and order, the Lord of the mind and the emotions. And for our sake, He wants our relationship with Him to be based on the firm foundation of the truth of His Word.

Trust Your Lover

Trust. That little word conjures up many mixed emotions and fears in our hearts. But trust is critical to the love connection and the healing of our aching places. Jesus wants you to rise to a higher level of trust in Him by way of His Holy Spirit. He will help you do so.

What is your part? Once you have trusted Jesus for salvation, ask Him to place in you a hunger and thirst for more of Him, a yearning for an intimacy beyond mere belief, ritual or habit. Ask Him to fill you with His Holy Spirit. Climb the ladder of trust, look down at your Love and hear Him say in tones of deepest love and reassurance, "Go ahead and jump. I'll catch you!"

In the next section we will discuss several specific ways we can trust our Lover to heal, fill and refill our aching places out of His endless bounty. In chapter 4 we will see how Jesus offers the opportunity many of us have longed for: to substitute a new and lovelier name for the names from our past that signify hurt and shame and prevent us from becoming all He intends for us to be.

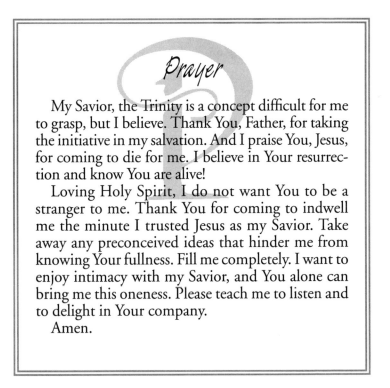

Prayer

My Savior, the Trinity is a concept difficult for me to grasp, but I believe. Thank You, Father, for taking the initiative in my salvation. And I praise You, Jesus, for coming to die for me. I believe in Your resurrection and know You are alive!

Loving Holy Spirit, I do not want You to be a stranger to me. Thank You for coming to indwell me the minute I trusted Jesus as my Savior. Take away any preconceived ideas that hinder me from knowing Your fullness. Fill me completely. I want to enjoy intimacy with my Savior, and You alone can bring me this oneness. Please teach me to listen and to delight in Your company.

Amen.

PART 2

TRUSTING THE ONE WHO LOVES YOU

4

He Gives You a New Name

Names can be fun and revealing. My given name was Barbara Janis, but as I grew up my family and friends all called me Bobbie. I had never thought much about my name, but when I was in my late teens and living in Washington, D.C., all that changed.

I was rooming with a good friend and working to earn enough money to further my education. My friend and I were both Christians, mature in some ways but not in others, and we enjoyed some zany and wonderful times together in the capital of our nation.

One evening we were invited to a chaperoned party at a nearby military base. For some crazy reason we decided to change our names for the event. After all, no one there would know us and we could pick names we had always liked.

"Roxanne!" my friend said, indicating her first choice.

"No," I laughed, "it's not you!"

She finally selected the name Lynn, and I decided to go with Jan, since it was part of my given name anyway and I liked it. Off we went to the party, practicing our new names over and over so we would not slip up.

"Lynn," I kept saying. "You're Lynn tonight."

"Jan, Jan, Jan—oh, I hope I can remember!" "Lynn" replied.

All evening we used our names with expertise and were immensely proud of ourselves. Little did I know I would

meet someone at the party who would end up figuring as
a major part of God's plan for my life. His name was Dave
McCray, and we began seeing each other on a regular basis
soon afterwards.

But it was nearly three months into this new relationship before I told Dave my real name.

"I'm really Bobbie," I told him, feeling a little foolish as
I explained my silly masquerade.

Dave looked at me for a moment, then shook his head.

"No," he responded, "you're Jan."

And I have been Jan ever since.

Jesus Knows Your Real Name

A lover often chooses a special name for the beloved, a
name of endearment or intimacy, or a name fitting a particular attribute or characteristic. Just so, Jesus has a new
name or names for each of us. An important step in trusting our Lover and allowing Him to heal our aching place
is accepting the new name or names He has for us.

In Isaiah 43:1 God says to you and me, "Do not fear, for
I have redeemed you; I have called you by name; you are
Mine!" Calling a person by her name implies personal
knowledge and, in this increasingly depersonalized world,
a sense of taking the trouble to care. For God to call us by
name means all that and more. It implies deep understanding, love and tenderness. How wonderful for each of
us to be called by name by the God of the universe—and,
even more, to know that His Son, Jesus, loves us enough
to give us our real names, names that fit!

Names in the Bible

In Bible times names were not given as casually as they
often are today. Names had meaning and significance. Fre-

quently a child was honored with a name her mother hoped she would become. Sometimes a child's name indicated a specific emotion or circumstance the mother or father was experiencing at the time of the child's birth. Joseph, for instance, sold into slavery by his brothers, named his first son *Manasseh,* which means "making to forget," because God had helped Joseph forget those painful memories. Joseph named his second son *Ephraim,* which means "fruitfulness." In Ephraim's birth Joseph celebrated God's blessing on himself and his family, even in a land of exile.

In several instances God actually changed someone's name because his or her old name no longer fit the person or circumstances. You remember Jacob, whose name meant "heel-catcher" or "supplanter" because of his status as a second son and the elaborate deception he and his mother concocted in order to steal the birthright and family blessing that belonged to Esau, his slightly older twin.

Jacob the supplanter endured many unpleasant events, some of them induced by his own deceitful nature, before he came to a place of humility and repentance before God. Finally the time came when he wrestled all night long, praying desperately to obtain God's blessing on his life. And at that point God changed his name from *Jacob,* the cocky supplanter, to *Israel,* which means "one who persists with God" or "a man clinging to God." God knew from Jacob's heart and actions that the old name no longer fit him.

The apostle Paul had been Saul of Tarsus, an educated Jew with all kinds of earthly reasons for pride. Saul killed the followers of Jesus with a passion. As a devout Pharisee, he thought he was doing God a service. Then Saul had an extraordinary meeting with Jesus on the road from Jerusalem to Damascus, and gradually acquired the name *Paul,* the Roman counterpart of his Jewish name. It means "of little consequence"—perhaps a reminder to Paul that he was never to succumb to human praise and honor but always give God the glory for his accomplishments.

Other characters mentioned in the New Testament also underwent name changes so they could see themselves more as Jesus saw them. Simon, the disciple, was one of these. Jesus had called Simon to follow Him and Simon responded. One day, as Jesus and His followers walked along the road, Jesus asked them who people thought He was. The disciples responded that many thought He was Elijah or Jeremiah or another of the prophets. Then Jesus posed the question that goes down in the history of the Church as the most important question of the age: "But who do you say that I am?" (Matthew 16:16).

"You are the Christ, the Son of the living God," Simon answered joyously, enthusiastically.

It was the right answer, and at that very moment Jesus changed Simon's name to *Peter,* which means "rock." Why? Because Jesus knew that the reality and truth of this confession would be the foundation on which the Church would be built. He also knew Peter would become the great shepherd and leader of that early Church.

Did Simon Peter see himself as a rock, especially after denying three times on the night before Jesus died that he knew Him? I doubt it. But Jesus saw Peter not as the impulsive, headstrong fisherman who declared great loyalty, then fell victim to human frailty. Jesus saw Peter's potential and bestowed this new name as a strong affirmation of the power of God that would work mightily through Peter. Jesus gave Peter a name that fit his confessed intention to follow his Lord to the end, and predicted his future participation in the Kingdom of God.

When we, like Peter, encounter Jesus by making the love connection, we must allow Him to give us a new name. Until we do, we may not fully trust Him as the Lover we need most.

Rejecting Wrong Names

Many of us carry around wrong names, either consciously or unconsciously, names that betray our aching places, names that do not fit our new relationship with our Lover and our new position in His Kingdom. Some of us carry more than one wrong name, and although we have experienced salvation and the filling of the Holy Spirit, even have made the love connection, we do not realize He can rid us of these "handles" that hurt.

Before we can accept the new name or names Jesus has chosen for us, we need to identify some of the old ones that hinder us from blossoming into the people He knows we really are. Do you already know the wrong names you need to destroy? They affect your relationship with Jesus and others, but may be so entrenched in you that their meanings have become part of your personality. They may seem natural, familiar, fitting with a coziness that makes you fear leaving them behind—even though you know they are deadly.

What are some of these names? They include *Unloved, Unworthy, Condemned* and *Inadequate.* Others are *Rejected, Confused, Depressed, Illogical, Insignificant, Hopeless* and *Failure.* We would also have to add *Defeated, Ugly, Trapped, Stupid, Wallflower, Shallow* and *Empty.*

Names like these, and others that pound in your spirit day after discouraging day, may have been reinforced in you over the years by faulty and harmful relationships—some not of your own choosing—that have brought damaging self-condemnation. The circumstances of your birth and present life may seem crushing, weighing you down with a sense of futility, a feeling that nothing will ever change, least of all you! And through it all, the wrong names you carry are quietly sabotaging the truth of who God says you are.

What can you do? Ask God to help you recognize, reject, give up and destroy those names. But before you do, you need a new name or names with which to replace them. Your new name comes from the Word and heart of God. Let's look in the next few pages at several names and the lives of women who have claimed them.

Your Name Is . . . *Loved*

How many times have you been told that Jesus loves you? If you were raised in the Church, you have not only heard it hundreds of times, but sung it as many! Even if you grew up outside the Church, the phrase *Jesus loves me, this I know* may be a sweet, comforting cliché from your childhood to hug when life gets fearsome. But despite the often saccharine reminders (even in the secular media!) that we are loved by God, we have become all too immune to this great truth. The love of God has become such a generalized, even popularized, concept that we have failed to claim personally the name He longs to give us—the name *Loved.* If you want to find the healing of your aching place and learn to trust your Lover with abandon, this truth has to get deep into your spirit: Your name is *Loved.*

The Bible affirms this fact on almost every page. From Genesis to Revelation we read the love story of a God whose creatures have used His gift of free choice to reject obedience, love and light in favor of sin, hate and darkness. We read of His plan to buy us back, to redeem us to Himself. His unfailing, unending and unconditional love resounds over and over in His dealings with Israel and in the personal lives of those who know Him.

God's love has nothing to do with our being lovable or worthy. It comes from a God who cared so much for His hurting children—who have made choices with devastating consequences—that He has gone to all lengths to reconcile them to His heart of love.

God could never excuse the sin that separated us from Him, but He could leave the adoration and glory of heaven and come to earth to deal a death blow to sin. He could allow Himself—the all-powerful, all-majestic God of the universe—to be squeezed into a baby's body and be born of a woman. Through His veins would run the blood that had to be shed in order for our sins to be forgiven, in order for us to be made right with Him. He preferred to die the agonizing and brutal death of crucifixion than to have us die in our sins without Him, never knowing we are loved.

Notice one vital fact: *He initiated and carried out this marvelous love in action, without our asking.* He did not wait until we got our act together. He knew we never could. Instead He demonstrated this unbelievable love in that while we were still in the middle of our sin, He gave His life for each of us (see Romans 5:8).

Who else could love like this? Who else would search us out and woo us and reveal His love over and over? Only God, through the Person of Jesus, our great Lover. No human being has ever loved or ever *could* love you or me in this unconditional, self-sacrificing way, because humanly speaking it is impossible. Only God's love is completely selfless, perfect, utterly without flaw or qualifications.

"I have loved you with an everlasting love," whispers your incomparable Lover (Jeremiah 31:3). His love is an accomplished fact, total and complete today. It does not measure sixty percent now with the promise of seventy percent when we improve a bit. Nor does it measure one hundred percent today, only to drop to fifty percent when we blow it tomorrow. You and I are loved one hundred percent *just as we are,* and this love will never decrease or fluctuate one iota.

How can this be? Because God's love for us is part of His unchanging character. He cannot stop loving us.

We are used to winning love, earning it through our behavior, intellect, good looks or personality. We are used to jumping through hoops to please people in hopes of receiving the love our aching places crave. We have the idea that if we can finally make ourselves pleasing enough, people will love us. This fallacy only makes our failures and imperfections appear more acute, and we end up living on a treadmill, never quite making it. When the truth of God's unconditional love finally floods our spirits and spills over into our daily existence, we will be free from jumping through hoops forever.

"But I can't comprehend fairy-tale love like that!" you say. And you are right. Our concept of God is so mixed up with emotions and painful experiences and the human interactions in our past that we cannot conceive of Him as being different from the people who have given and withdrawn their love from us over the years. Our very definition of the word *love* may need to be altered so that our past will not hinder our new relationship with our Lover.

How Do I Accept My New Name of *Loved*?

The key to accepting your new name, *Loved,* is not in understanding it, because you never will, but in making another leap of trust based on your love connection with Jesus through the Holy Spirit. Do not allow yourself to get bogged down in questions like "Why does He love me?" or "How *can* He love me?" The fact is, He does!

Returning to the story of Peter will help you grasp how the Spirit can implant the reality of His love in your life, giving you a new name once and for all. Remember when Jesus changed Simon's name to Peter? Simon had just stated the true identity of Jesus—that He was the Son of the living God. But Jesus did not want Simon Peter in his human pride to misuse that information, so He explained to His impetuous friend that "flesh and blood did not reveal this to you, but my Father who is in heaven" (Matthew 16:17).

In other words, Peter did not just pick up this profound truth by being around Jesus and seeing the miracles—just as you will never grasp the reality of your new name, *Loved,* by growing up in the Church or performing some given ritual. The very Spirit of God imparted this truth to Peter, and helped him make a huge leap of trust that would transform his relationship with Jesus.

The same Holy Spirit must reveal to you the unconditional love of Jesus, the gift that changes your name to *Loved.* In and of yourself you cannot comprehend it, even though your intellect may believe it. But Jesus, your Lover, wants you to experience His love in your inner spirit. This is where it needs to pour over your raw aching place, until the ache begins to respond to His divine healing balm.

When will the Holy Spirit reveal the love of Jesus to us? When we ask Him, as my friend Patti did.

Her Name Was Depressed

I met Patti through a Bible sharing group, and I enjoyed her zest and enthusiasm for Jesus. She was one of the most honest people I had ever met, loving Jesus with a passion as the Lover of her life.

But it had not always been so. A few years before, Patti had been a self-described "nominal" believer, disconnected from God except through the prayers of her mother, a strong Christian. When Patti's sons were about seven and five, Patti slipped into a severe depression. Her doctor put her on an antidepressant, but the grayness persisted.

"Some days I couldn't remember if I had fed the boys their breakfast or not," she told me. "I felt detached from everything."

Desperate, she even took her mother's suggestion and tried reading the Bible and praying, but she could not concentrate enough to make any headway.

"Some nights I would stand at the window after everyone had gone to bed, looking up into the dark sky," she said. "I wished God would just let me die so I could be out of my misery."

Finally Patti felt she could cope with her depression no longer. Nothing seemed to release her from her dark abyss. One day as she went about the routine chores of mothering and homemaking, she felt herself making what seemed like an involuntary decision in her heart.

"All day long," she recalled, "I kept saying to myself that this day would be the last one of my life. I felt my children would be better off without me."

But in her despair Patti made a final plea to God.

"Please help me today, God, if You're there!" she screamed. "Send someone this very day to help me, if You are real!"

In the early afternoon someone knocked on Patti's door. When she opened it, a woman she did not know burst out joyfully, "I've come to tell you how much Jesus loves you!"

God had answered Patti's prayer. And He had not merely sent someone to deter Patti from her suicide pact, thereby proving His reality. That would have been amazing enough. But true to His extravagant nature, He lavished His tenderness on His lost child by instructing His messenger to give Patti His love—the very invitation she needed desperately to keep on living.

Patti's crisis of depression opened her heart to a longing for God she never knew existed. Probably her mother had been praying for that day when Patti not only yielded to Jesus but began to hunger and thirst for Him.

That day Patti asked God to show Himself to her. He did—in a direct, personal and unmistakable way—and changed her name from *Depressed* to *Loved*.

An encounter Patti had, which took place after she and her family moved to the east coast of Florida, showed me the depth of the change that had taken place.

After much prayer, Patti decided Jesus wanted her to conduct a beach ministry. During the day she walked along the beach in Fort Lauderdale, Bible in hand. A custom-made T-shirt became her uniform. On one side it said *Who Cares?* in huge letters. On the other side, in equally large letters: *Jesus Cares!*

One day a young man came up to her and yelled, "Who cares? I really like your shirt, lady! Where'd you get it?"

Before she could answer, he went on, "Who cares? That's the truth! *Nobody* cares, that's who."

Patti could see he was high on something. She turned around with a grin and showed him the back of her shirt.

His expression changed abruptly. Grabbing her arm, he yelled, "Jesus cares? Are you one of those Jesus freaks? I don't like this shirt now, lady." His grip on her arm tightened. His voice was slurred and angry. "Get off our beach! You got no right coming around here wearing that shirt."

Patti looked him in the eye and said softly, "Listen, there was a time in my life when I thought Jesus didn't care, either. I had two little boys, but my life was so full of pain that I decided to make that day my last one on this earth."

His grip loosened. Patti prayed within for the help of the Holy Spirit.

"In hopelessness and desperation I cried out to God," she continued, "and told Him to send someone to help me if He really cared, because I couldn't hang on any longer."

The young man let go of Patti's arm.

"God *did* send someone that very day. She's the one who told me how much Jesus cares. God saved my life, and I promised Him I would never stop telling people that Jesus *does* care, and that He loves them deeply and can help them."

The young man stared into Patti's face. She did not know what to expect. "Do you think Jesus could ever love me?" he asked at last.

With the breeze caressing her hair and the love of Jesus flowing from her spirit, Patti sat down on the sand with the young man and shared the riches of the grace of God through His Son. Her Lover was using her as a vessel of His tenderness to show others His love as well.

In order to begin dumping your own wrong names and receive the name *Loved,* you must ask the Holy Spirit of God to plant this authentic truth in your spirit. Only He can do it. He is waiting, with love and longing in His heart, to hear your voice and call you *Loved.*

Your Name Is . . . Forgiven

Jesus wants to give you another name besides *Loved* to replace the wrong names you have been carrying around. That name is *Forgiven.*

It is easy to see, just as we discovered with the name *Loved,* that we may believe in our heads that we are forgiven, but never appropriate that fact for the healing of our aching place. We may realize intellectually that God knew in advance we would sin, so He sent Jesus to die a sacrificial death on the cross, paying for our sins. Still we fall into the trap of thinking that our performance causes us to deserve His forgiveness, and we miss the point, thus blocking a deeper relationship with our Lover.

To be named *Forgiven* is a blessing undeserved. God's forgiveness has nothing to do with our merit and everything to do with His grace, His undeserved favor in the face of our sin. God's forgiveness is connected to His love; the two are inextricably woven together into one beautiful piece of fabric. We are named *Forgiven* because His love sent Jesus to the cross, completely on His own initiative.

The prophet Micah used the metaphor of the world's great oceans in explaining the vastness of God's forgiveness. He said, "Thou wilt cast all their sins into the depths of the sea" (7:19).

What a wonderful picture! The sea is immense and endless, virtually bottomless. And Micah tells us that our sin, once confessed, is swallowed up in the immense, endless, bottomless sea of God's forgiveness and forgetfulness. It is gone, never to resurface. He threw it there Himself, and we need never fear that one day it will wash up on the shore! The experience of real forgiveness and receiving the new name *Forgiven* should wash away forever many wrong names you are carrying.

Several years ago I spoke at a women's conference where I met a young woman named Anne, who had been diagnosed recently with Hodgkin's disease. I was drawn to her immediately by two things: her closeness in age to one of our daughters and her deep sensitivity to Jesus, whom she had come to know as an adult. Raised in a family in which Christ was not honored or even recognized, Anne had never, in her words, "received much father or mother love." Both of her parents had too many needs of their own to address the needs of their children. Anne began drinking at an early age and experimented with drugs and promiscuity.

Then a friend at work introduced Anne to Jesus. It was like a dream come true. Jesus' love gave her a new identity, a new life, a new purpose. She went back to school and eventually became a counselor in a state prison.

But as Anne listened to the messages I gave the weekend we met, she asked me to pray with her—not for healing from her Hodgkin's disease, but for a more intimate relationship with Jesus.

"I get this nagging feeling now and then that not all my sins are really forgiven," she told me. "It comes over me like a cloud and I say to myself, *Who do you think you are? Someday you will stand before God and discover that some of your sins were too horrible for Him to forgive!*"

I realized almost immediately what was wrong. Each and every day Anne was carrying the name *Guilty.* She loved

Jesus and did not doubt the validity of His cleansing blood, but she was overwhelmed by her own shame and unworthiness. She had never forgiven herself for her past, and she thought Jesus saw her in the same way she saw herself.

"Anne," I said, "Jesus has already forgiven you of all your sin. But each time He tries to hold you close, you pull away because you don't feel worthy."

Anne nodded, so I continued, "You must forgive yourself."

Then I asked Anne a question that got her full attention. "Anne, you're not holier than Jesus, are you?"

Her eyes darted toward mine. "No, of course not!" she exclaimed.

"Then if He, in all His holiness, has forgiven you, can't you forgive yourself?"

We prayed, and Anne asked Jesus to help her be able to forgive herself. It was a first step toward receiving her new name, *Forgiven*.

I continued to pray for Anne when I returned home after that conference, not only that she would accept her new name, but also for healing of the Hodgkin's disease. Anne knew Jesus was able to heal her, but to my surprise and delight she seemed more interested in making Him her Love than in focusing on the difficult treatments and sleeplessness she endured as the cancer progressed. Anne was falling in love with Jesus over and over in her daily walk; and her letters, often written during the painful night watches, were poignant, breathtaking accounts of the love relationship she was enjoying with her Lord. She radiated joy and contentment, and used her artistic ability to paint me a miniature of roses centered in greenery with these words prominently displayed: *I Am Forgiven*.

Anne is in heaven with her Lover today, but while I grieved the loss of this friend, I was reassured to remember that not even death could "separate [Anne] from the love of God, which is in Christ Jesus our Lord" (Romans 8:39).

"Your sins are forgiven you for His name's sake," says 1 John 2:12. Your name is not only *Loved;* it is *Forgiven.*

Your Name Is . . . Cherished

Jesus longs to give you one other name to replace the wrong ones you have acquired for yourself: *Cherished.*
What is the difference between *Loved* and *Cherished?*
To love, according to the *American Heritage Dictionary,* is "to feel strong affection or attachment to another person based on regard or shared experiences or interests." To cherish means "to hold dear; to treat with affection or tenderness. . . . to keep fondly in mind." To cherish implies not only *feeling* love, but *acting* to serve the beloved and *sensing* how the beloved gives the lover joy.

"How beautiful and how delightful you are, my love," rejoiced the bridegroom in Solomon's beautiful allegory of Christ and the Church (Song of Solomon 7:6). That is the way Jesus feels about you!

God's cherishing is revealed in the way He holds you dear, supplying "all your needs according to His riches in glory in Christ Jesus" (Philippians 4:19). The lover who cherishes the beloved never forgets him or her. In Isaiah 49:15 we hear our Lover saying, "I will not forget you." And the Bible tells how God's love for you, and yours for Him, gives Him joy. Zephaniah 3:17 says that your Lover "will exult over you with joy, He will be quiet in His love, He will rejoice over you with shouts of joy." That range of feeling shows that He enjoys your company!

God's cherishing is also revealed in the way He acts toward you.

Unlike a human lover, who may profess undying love one moment and lash out in hurtful speech the next, your Lover will never treat you in a way that is outside His nature of love. In Jeremiah 31:3 we hear Him say, "I have loved you with an everlasting love; therefore I have drawn you with lovingkindness." Even when He must teach you new lessons in obedience, or reprove you as a Father, He will always do so in the context of cherishing.

God delights in listening to you, in crying with you, in laughing with you (see Psalm 4:3; 34:17; 126 [the whole psalm]; Proverbs 15:29; 1 John 5:14; John 11:33, 35; Job 8:21). He relishes talking with you (see Deuteronomy 5:24; Jeremiah 12:1) and savors each word you share with Him. He is anxious to let you know of His pride and joy in you (look again at Zephaniah 3:17), loves comforting you in sorrow and lifting you up when you are down (see Psalm 3:3; 147:6; John 14:18).

God never sees you as unworthy or inadequate or ugly. He loathes the wrong names you have acquired for yourself, desiring to unglue you from them and hold you close while He smashes them to bits.

You are *Cherished* by the God of all creation, the Maker of the universe, the Savior of the world.

All You Have to Do Is Ask

What name, either overt or subtle, is hindering you from accepting the truth of who you are in Jesus, your Love? He longs to free you from the wrong names you have picked up along the way.

One way to do this is to reflect over past experiences that have damaged you. If they seem nebulous, ask His Spirit to bring to your mind the ones you need to deal with so that you can be healed. As He does bring them to mind, write down the name or names that come out of the experience.

Now look at your list. Those names are a lie. Jesus wants to deliver you from them and from their effects in your life. He wants to give you your new names.

How can you receive them? Cry out to God.

That is what Jabez did. A descendant of Judah mentioned in 1 Chronicles 4, Jabez was named "pain" by his mother because she suffered greatly at his birth. But verse 10 says Jabez cried out to God, asking Him to break the curse of the name, to bless him, to be with him, to keep him from harm and to see to it that he would not be in pain. Jabez recognized that this hurtful name would affect his relationship with God and with everyone else. Unwilling to live out that cursed name any longer, he asked God to deliver him. "And God granted him what he requested" (verse 10).

God can and will do the same for you. You can live and die with the wrong name, but Jesus paid an enormous price to give you your new one. By His Spirit you can be delivered from your old name and receive your new one.

Ask God to plant in your spirit the reality of your new name or names. Then take your list of wrong names and destroy it, rip it to pieces. Now look into the face of Jesus, your Lover, and hear Him say, "You are Loved, you are Forgiven, you are Cherished."

Getting used to your new names will take time. Satan, your enemy, does not want you to accept these names because he knows they will free you from his tricks. So he will throw the old names in your face again and again, harassing you with shame and accusation about past failures. Refuse to play his game. No matter how his nasty tactics make you feel, tell him firmly, "That old name doesn't fit me anymore. Jesus has given me a new one, so leave me alone, in Jesus' name!"

In James 4:7 we are told, "Resist the devil and he will flee from you." That same verse reads this way in *The Message:* "Yell a loud *no* to the Devil and watch him scamper." You will have to practice using your new name and resisting Satan, but Jesus is a faithful Lover who has promised to stand by you all the way.

Does this new relationship and love connection with Jesus still seem unattainable? Does knowing Jesus through the Holy Spirit still seem vague? Read on. Your Lover is waiting to transform your whole life, just as He has changed your name.

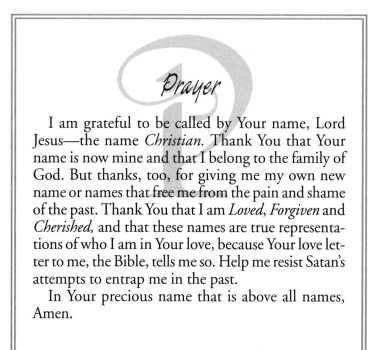

Prayer

I am grateful to be called by Your name, Lord Jesus—the name *Christian.* Thank You that Your name is now mine and that I belong to the family of God. But thanks, too, for giving me my own new name or names that free me from the pain and shame of the past. Thank You that I am *Loved, Forgiven* and *Cherished,* and that these names are true representations of who I am in Your love, because Your love letter to me, the Bible, tells me so. Help me resist Satan's attempts to entrap me in the past.

In Your precious name that is above all names, Amen.

5

He Is Your Source of Self-Esteem

Shortly after I accepted Jesus as my Savior, I met a girl at school who was also a believer. We became friends and attended many of the same youth functions together. But one of the best parts of our friendship was the privilege of visiting in her home. The whole family was Jesus-centered, and I always felt His presence when I was with them.

I was particularly drawn to my friend's attractive twenty-year-old sister, Ruth. Looking back on it now, I realize Ruth was not especially pretty by the world's standards, but she radiated a beautiful confidence and joy. She always took time with her sister and me, listening and giving advice. She never failed to include Jesus in our conversations, and when I heard her speak of Him, I could tell she knew Him on a first-name basis.

One Sunday while I was visiting, Ruth was getting ready to go with a young adult group to visit shut-ins. She sang a little Gospel chorus as she gathered up her Bible and purse, then turned to give her mom a big hug. Giggling, she gave her sister and me each a big kiss. We all stood still for a moment after she left; then her mother said something I will never forget.

"That Ruth!" she laughed. "She is so in love with Jesus!"

I had never heard anyone use that expression before, *so in love with Jesus.* The words kept ringing in my mind. Was it being in love with Jesus that made Ruth so special, so sure of herself?

Looking for Self-Esteem in All the Wrong Places

Sure of herself. Confident. Full of self-respect. That was Ruth. Those qualities she evidenced so readily are components of a commodity desired by every human being—a commodity that has special bearing on a woman's aching place. It is called self-esteem.

In recent years psychologists, sociologists, educators and theologians have written reams about self-esteem and its role in the development of human wholeness and well-being. The search for self-esteem leads men and women to seek significance, self-validation and a place to "shine." The sources from which women seek these goods most often include our mates, our children, our performance in the home and out of it. Perfection in and of itself—as wives, mothers, homemakers, career women—can become a goal as we seek recognition for who and what we are.

But as most of us discover sooner or later, the search for self-esteem in our human strength takes us to all the wrong places. The roadway ends up littered with failed dreams and decayed expectations. They haunt our memories and overflow our aching places. Old patterns and habits defeat us; generational cycles of negative behavior persist. We learn eagerly how to jump through society's hoops—and our own—in the hope of gaining attention to boost our self-respect. And we trip and fall again and again. Each time our tender self-esteem takes another blow, eventually atrophying into uselessness and even self-destruction.

Through all our searching, Jesus, our Lover, woos us from the world's empty sources of self-esteem to a new or renewed confidence in Him as our "all in all." Here again His Spirit must lead us to the truth of who we are in Him. He knows every road we have traveled in search of a way to fill the self-esteem void in our aching places. He knows every substitution we have made for a source. And He longs to show us His way, to encourage us not to settle for less than He intended in our relationship with Him.

Jesus knows that if we rely on ourselves, on others or on the world's costly substitutes in order to supply and replenish our self-esteem, we will stop short of the intimacy and joy the love connection can offer to touch and heal the aching places in our spirits. We need to plant our fragile selves firmly on the fact that He is equipped to be our complete source of self-esteem.

Picture in your mind a poised princess, comfortable with who she is, comfortable with her heritage, comfortable in her standing with the people around her. Why is she at ease? Because she is created in the image of her father, the king, and because she knows that all his resources and connections are at her disposal. Her standing is secure because her relationship to her father is unquestioned.

If we have made the love connection with Jesus, our relationship to the King of kings is also unquestioned. And we can be equally at ease, poised and comfortable with who we are because Jesus tells us that "in Him [we] have been made complete" (Colossians 2:10).

I have heard this truth expounded many times for single women, but all women need to incorporate it into their spirits. Only in Jesus do we become whole, satisfied and full. Our relationship with Him was never intended to be a partial fulfillment of our identity, and it was certainly never designed as a supplemental policy to make up for the gaps in our relationships with our husbands, children or co-workers.

Jesus means to be—and must be—the entire and total determinant and source of our self-esteem. We can start to appropriate this truth in our lives by examining who or what we are clinging to as the source of our worth. The story of Leah, found in Genesis 29, will help us look at four major routes toward which the world directs us in our search for self-esteem.

1. The Appearance Route

Spiritual conflicts are often triggered by rejection, and Leah was a woman whose life was riddled with rejection and loss. In her journey toward self-esteem, she ultimately made a choice, discovering not only that she was on the wrong road, but the means by which to make an about-face.

You remember the story of Jacob and Esau, the twins whose competition for an inheritance we mentioned in the last chapter. (See Genesis 25 for their complete story.) This is the same Jacob whose name was later changed to reflect his new relationship with God. In the various cultural economies of Old Testament times, the oldest son normally received the birthright blessing and certain other material advantages. But since Esau was older than his twin by only a few minutes, Jacob felt cheated.

God already had told the twins' mother, Rebekah, that one day Esau would serve Jacob (see Genesis 25:23). It is often difficult, however, to wait for God to act, so Jacob and Rebekah deceived the boys' father, Isaac, into giving his dying blessing to Jacob.

Naturally Esau was furious when he discovered the deception, but custom would not allow his father to undo the damage. Rebekah, realizing Jacob's life was in danger, acted quickly, convincing her husband that Jacob should leave home and seek a wife from among the eligible women on her side of the family. Isaac agreed, and Jacob fled to Haran, to the home of Laban, Rebekah's brother.

In a beautiful story of love at first sight, Jacob happened upon Rachel, Laban's younger daughter, as he neared the family homestead. She had come to water her father's herd, and Jacob, when he comprehended who she was, was overcome by emotion. He helped her with her task and actually ended up kissing her, a pleasure normally reserved in their culture until after marriage. The only explanation is that Jacob was smitten, enraptured, filled with bliss.

Rachel took him home to meet the family that very day. The Bible says Jacob loved Rachel and agreed to work for his uncle Laban for seven years to earn her hand in marriage.

Enter Leah, stage left. This is how Laban's older daughter is introduced in Genesis 29:17: "Leah's eyes were weak, but Rachel was beautiful of form and face."

How would you like that as the only description of you in the family chronicles? Your eyes are weak but your little sister is beautiful! Leah probably had to squint in order to see, and to add insult to this affliction, she had a younger sibling who turned heads the moment she entered a room.

Has a similar situation shaped your life? Our culture has always placed far greater value on the outside appearance of women than on the shape of their characters. Magazines, television, books, advertisements and conversation all scream, "Looks matter!" The media instills a not-so-subtle view that our success, fulfillment, happiness and, ultimately, self-esteem are derived in large measure from our looks.

More teens in America suffer from eating disorders than most people imagine. Many come from Christian homes. They are trying to live up to a standard placed on them by society, and sometimes their families.

Face it: All of us are told regularly that our bodies must fit a certain pattern and shape. If they do not, we are unacceptable. We are encouraged to do anything and everything to avoid wrinkles and the appearance of aging, since the weathered face of a woman bent over from age and hard work is repulsive to many of us. The majority of women in the Western world, Christians included, find no joy in the successive stages of life because of what time does to our outer shells.

Things have not changed much since Leah's time.

Which takes us back to our story. Jacob, head over heels in love with beautiful Rachel, worked for seven years to earn her as his wife. And on the sidelines Leah, growing older and plainer with each passing day, must have wondered if a life of loneliness loomed on her horizon.

Finally it was time for the wedding. The Bible tells us Jacob went to his uncle and said, "Give me my wife, for my time is completed, that I may go in to her" (29:21). Laban's next move was an expected one: He "gathered all the men of the place, and made a feast" (29:22).

Weddings, then as now, were joyful celebrations, and Hebrew custom dictated that they could last many days, accompanied by banquets, laughter, much wine and great merriment. Because the groom was not allowed to see his wife's face until the marriage was consummated, she wore a veil during the whole affair.

At last Jacob and his bride were alone in their tent. We can only imagine Jacob's anticipation: He had waited and worked seven years for the pleasure of being with Rachel.

There was only one problem. Genesis 29:23 indicates that after all the feasting, "in the evening . . . [Laban] took his daughter *Leah,* and brought her to [Jacob]; and Jacob went in to her" (italics mine). Whether her veil stayed on all night, or the tent was excessively dim, or Jacob was pretty well intoxicated, we are not sure. Maybe it was a combination of all three. But Jacob apparently did not discover until morning that he was married to the wrong girl.

The Bible tells us what he said to Laban. In fact, he must have thundered it: "What is this you have done to me? Was it not for Rachel that I served with you? Why then have you deceived me?" (29:25). Sneaky Jacob, the supplanter, now experienced firsthand what it felt like to be deceived.

But Laban did not apologize. He explained to Jacob, probably in a reasonable tone, that the older daughter had to be married off before the younger one, and asked Jacob to "complete the bridal week of this one, and we will give you the other also for the service which you shall serve with me for another seven years" (29:27).

What choice did Jacob have? He did as he was told, and by the end of the week he had two wives—and another seven years of work ahead!

It is a temptation to feel sorry for the lovebirds, Jacob and Rachel. Still, they ultimately got to be together, which is what they wanted, even though they faced many years of heartache in their future.

My heart goes out to Leah, who must have felt unbelievably used—unwanted, forced on a man who loved another woman, feeling unattractive already. She knew full well that her father had resorted to trickery in order to pawn her off—and gotten free labor out of her "sale" in the process. Leah knew the customs of her tribe; she may have known for some time that Laban intended to deceive Jacob. But even if she had grave objections to the whole plot, it would not have mattered: She was obligated to obey her father.

For all we know, Leah may have spent the entire wedding night listening to Jacob whisper sweet nothings intended for Rachel. Can you imagine those hours for Leah? Can you imagine fearing to speak, lest your voice be recognized? Can you imagine knowing that every touch from Jacob was meant for Rachel, yet still feeling obligated to respond? There are many kinds of humiliation, but this one has to be high on the "ten-worst" list! The seeds of Leah's loss of self-esteem had multiplied and taken deeper root.

Few women have endured Leah's particular agony, but most of us know what it means to be rejected for one reason or another because of our appearance. Those of us who have made the love connection with Jesus need to stop using the world's standard for measuring success in this matter of appearance. Instead we must adopt the biblical view.

What is that? The Bible tells us that God wants us to take care of our bodies because they house His precious Holy Spirit (see 1 Corinthians 3:16–17; 6:19). We should also lead the way in healthy eating, for the Bible offers many guidelines about nutrition. (That is a topic for another book!) As for taking healthy pride in the way we present ourselves, of course that is biblical, too. We who belong to the Lord are His representatives and should look our best.

But the world's view stretches these healthy principles into obsessions—obsessions we must resist. We cannot allow ourselves to derive our self-esteem from appearance alone; we are far more than faces and body shapes. As believers, and especially as believers who have made an intimate love connection with Jesus through the Holy Spirit, we bear the light of Jesus inside us. Our real beauty comes from allowing His light to shine from us like stars in a dark sky.

No one is more beautiful than a woman in love with Jesus and drawing her lifeblood from Him daily. Since "we have received, not the spirit of the world, but the Spirit who is from God" (1 Corinthians 2:12), we must make sure the Holy Spirit, not the world, shapes our identity and self-esteem.

Leah did not know Jesus; she was not connected with God through the Holy Spirit, as we are. But she was a believer in the one true God of the Old Testament. As she moved into the next phase of her life, adjusting to the festering marital bed of anger and rejection her father had set up for her, she could not know that the faulty routes she would try in her search for self-esteem would eventually lead her to an encounter with her true Love.

2. The Male-Female Relationship Route

And so began Leah's—and Jacob's and Rachel's—married life. As the old saying goes, "Two's company, three's a crowd."

Despite her social standing as the older daughter and sister in a respected family, Leah was definitely the third party in a crowded household of newlyweds.

If ever a woman had reason to doubt the male-female relationship route as a road to self-esteem, it was Leah. She had been used by her father to get seven extra years of work from Jacob. Now she was being used by Jacob, too. The Bible says Jacob "loved Rachel more than Leah," but that evidently did not keep him out of Leah's tent. She provided him with sons, the crown of a man's status in that culture. And in that Middle Eastern setting, Leah did not spend her days sipping wine and eating dates. She undoubtedly made an important contribution to the family's housekeeping chores and livelihood.

We will discuss the role of children in Leah's search for self-esteem in the next section. Right now, however, imagine how often she must have analyzed Jacob's touch, his glances, his attitude toward her, all the while looking for validation, for significance, for a sense that he valued her. Every time she bore his child, or accomplished a task he assigned her or prepared him a wonderful meal, she must have thought, *Maybe now Jacob will love me the way he loves Rachel.* Yet there is no biblical indication that Jacob ever fell in love with Leah as he had with Rachel.

He apparently honored her as his wife and the mother of his children, and when she died he buried her in the family tomb with Abraham, Sarah, Isaac and Rebekah (see Genesis 49:31). But, humanly speaking, any woman who has ever loved a man or desired his love knows that friendship and honor, while necessary and helpful to a successful marriage, are no substitute for the exclusive romantic love of your mate.

In a good marriage the husband can be a wonderful instrument of God to help nurture self-esteem in his wife. According to Ephesians 5:21–33 and 1 Peter 3:7, God has given each husband an important role in the marriage relationship: He is to bring his spouse into a deeper realization of God's goodness and mercy by modeling Jesus' servant heart of love, intimate knowledge and cherishing.

I appreciate the fact that Dave has never found it necessary to compete for the place of the Lover of my soul. He is supportive of my love relationship with Jesus, and recognizes my need (and his own) for submission to the one Lover who can be all in all to both of us. Dave and I have learned this pattern of relating to each other and to our Lord through trial and error, heartache and renewal, but Jesus has been faithful.

Can Dave touch my aching place? No, nor can I touch his. But he is often used by my great Lover to encourage me back to a special relationship of healing and refilling.

A husband can never be your complete source of self-esteem, even if he loves you dearly. He is human, as you are; and while his compliments or attention may seem like temporary salve on your wounded spirit, he does not have the ability to touch the aching place in your spirit in a way that offers lasting relief or deep-down joy.

God knew that Jacob could not be Leah's source. He also knew that only as Leah grew in intimacy with her heavenly Lover could she relate to the people in her life without harassing them or smothering them or demanding that they meet her every need.

It is the same with us. Only as we experience Jesus' total acceptance can we be free to accept our husbands, our children and our parents, and work for their personal growth as well as our own.

3. The Motherhood Route

Just as God designed the human body and called it good, and just as He designed marriage and called it good, so He designed the institution of parenting and encouraged Adam and Eve to pursue it (see Genesis 1 and 2). But He never intended for any of these wonderful gifts to become our sole source of self-esteem or an idol for our spirits to adore.

Yet how easily we women allow mothering to become an unhealthy reservoir of the love and attention we crave in our aching places! Leah was no exception.

Shortly after the weddings, Jacob, Leah and Rachel came face to face with a sticky situation. Leah could bear children; Rachel could not.

Infertility brings great pain to women in all cultures, but in the Middle East it signifies a huge loss of significance, a disgrace, even a curse. In that region of the world, a woman's self-esteem is tied closely to her ability to conceive and bear children, and to this day Jewish women gather at the tomb of Rachel, just outside Bethlehem, to pray for their own deliverance from barrenness.

Now Leah had a tool to use against the emotional abuse and rejection inflicted by her father and (however inadvertently) by Jacob. And she now had another route to try in her quest for self-esteem: She had no trouble at all producing one child after another.

Hey, look at me! she must have thought as she observed Rachel's dilemma. *I can give Jacob something you can't!*

What's more, Leah's first three children were sons, which in that culture were infinitely preferable to daughters, and which increased her temporary sense of well-being. The names Leah gave her boys indicated the roles she expected them to play in her journey toward self-esteem. The first she named Reuben, which means "Because the Lord has seen my affliction." The second name, Simeon, signaled her understanding that the Lord had heard she was unloved and blessed her with a son. The third name, Levi, was a pathetic flickering of hope: "Now this time my husband will become attached to me, because I have borne him three sons" (Genesis 29:34).

But Leah's relationship with Jacob did not change. He still loved Rachel better. Leah should have been able to win his love and admiration, since she was doing for him what Rachel could not. So why was this route failing?

Several years ago at a prayer retreat, I met a young woman in her mid-twenties who asked if she could speak to me about an important prayer request. We met at the retreat center cafeteria and sat down for a cup of coffee.

"What's on your heart?" I asked after we had shared some small talk.

She was nervous, and although I could tell she loved Jesus, I saw deep sadness in her eyes and heard a haunting loneliness in her voice. She told me she had one little girl, but wanted another child desperately and had been unable to get pregnant. Would I pray for her?

I get many such requests, and ordinarily I love being in prayer partnership with such women. I have held the answers to many of those prayers in my arms—darling babies whose mothers thought they would never be, precious little ones who came about through miraculous conceptions or adoptions.

But I sensed something in my spirit concerning this young woman and began asking questions about her husband and his feelings about having more children. At first she was hesitant to talk much about him. But as I encouraged her, she poured out the story of his abusive background. He was a professing Christian now and had never abused her or their daughter physically, but the emotional abuse she endured was taking a toll. He seemed unable to give or receive intimate love, was possessive and discouraged her from close contact with her family or close friendships with women. He often abused her verbally in front of their daughter. He wanted his wife's undivided attention but criticized her appearance, her mannerisms, her housekeeping and the way she was raising their child.

"Is he willing to get help?" I asked. I had to know.

She shook her head and stared at the floor.

It was a situation that screamed for long-term counseling, prayer and change. This dear young woman was willing, but was hesitant to share the situation with her pastor because she feared it would lessen his respect for her husband. I told her the pastor needed to know, and she agreed to make this a start. I ached for her. What had she been like before the erosion of her self-esteem?

Before we parted that day I held her hands in mine and looked into her teary eyes.

"Why do you want another baby when your situation is so delicate and uncertain?" I asked gently.

"Because my little girl loves me," she wept into her napkin, "and I want someone to love me."

Leah, like this young woman, had unknowingly decided to make the act of bearing children—and, eventually, their accomplishments and love for her—major sources of self-esteem and happiness. She hoped by so doing to relieve the hurt and lack of emotional intimacy in her life. She wanted to fill an emotional and psychological hole that was getting deeper every day.

If only Leah and my young friend had known that God alone can fill such a void!

Perhaps you are not in so desperate a situation as either of these women. But it is still tempting to make your children your main source of self-esteem. How they look, how they dress, what they accomplish socially, academically, artistically and even spiritually can become vicarious sources of pride and secondhand bouquets. After all, you are the one who engineered this success!

Once again you are making the mistake of misusing a good gift from God to boost the sagging, aching place in your spirit.

And there is still one more common highway women travel in the search for self-esteem.

4. The Accomplishment Route

Leah's journey toward significance actually followed a confused road map that included all three of the false routes we have already explored: the appearance route, the male-female relationship route and the motherhood route. All of them intersected again and again in Leah's life, as they frequently do today.

Similarly the accomplishment route wove its way around Leah's map. For her, having children was an accomplishment. It increased and enhanced her duties in her roles as a wife and homemaker—legitimate (if not always valued and honored) roles in that period of history.

The accomplishment route is one Satan has used with tremendous success in more recent generations to fool women into thinking they are rich in self-esteem. The need to perform—whether in the academic, artistic, religious or business realm—drives many women into frantic rat races that destroy their health and relationships and eclipse their desperate need for intimacy with their great Love, Jesus.

My friend Fran was articulate and zealous when she shared with me her desire to be accepted by a large mission organization for service in a foreign country. She had her goals all laid out, and I sensed she would not stop until they had all been realized.

Not long after I first met her, I heard she had indeed been accepted by the mission board and was heading abroad for language study. Soon afterward she took her first assignment, and we corresponded during her initial four years out of the United States.

When Fran came home on furlough, she called to see if we could have lunch. I was delighted to see her again.

"How are things going with you?" I asked.

She showed me a schedule she had worked out for her time at home. It overwhelmed me.

"How will you get all this done?" I asked in disbelief.

"I know it's ambitious," she admitted with a smile, "but I just hope I don't have to cancel anything on the list."

We talked about her work further as we ate. Finally I decided to steer our conversation into an area I felt we needed to discuss.

"Fran," I began hesitantly, "Jesus doesn't want you to kill yourself while you're home on furlough. Isn't coming home also supposed to be a time of renewal and refreshing for you?"

We spent the afternoon in conversation and prayer about intimacy with Jesus (although I am sure our lunch was intended to encompass about an hour on Fran's agenda for the day!) and what He desires from those of us who love and serve Him. Fran, I learned, had a drive to perform and was definitely "do-oriented."

Wanting to understand the root of this drive, I asked about her childhood and family connections. "Did your parents push you to perform?"

Fran thought for a minute. "No, they didn't. My father was a hard-working man who took care of his family but didn't communicate much with us children. Mom was fine, but as I look back on it now, neither of them spent much time affirming us or building us up. They didn't belittle us, either; they just took care of us."

"What about school? Did you do well?"

That question opened the dam, and Fran began to pour out her heart.

"I was never pretty in high school," she confided, "but I realized I had a good mind and made excellent grades."

I disagreed with her about her looks; I thought she was beautiful! But I pressed on. "Did you receive praise at home for your good grades?"

"No," she smiled, "but I began to affirm myself."

Fran went on to tell me that she had come to see her good grades and academic ability as her avenue to succeed, to boost her self-esteem, to feel significant. When she received Jesus into her life, she transferred this vehicle of approval onto her relationship with Him. She was a good academic performer and now she felt a compulsion to perform well for Jesus, often taking on more than she was able to do, yet always fearing it was not enough.

From the expression on Fran's face that day, I could tell she had buried this truth in her spirit for many years. It is hard to accept the reality that no service we can render our Lover is greater than building our relationship with Him.

"But," you protest, "the Bible says we are to go, tell, do!"

Absolutely. But all of what we do must grow out of our relational intimacy. Our service is the overflow of what we hear and learn in our close union with God.

Verses 8 and 9 of Ephesians 2 are familiar—the core of our belief that salvation comes by God's grace only, not by anything we do: "For by grace you have been saved through faith; and that not of yourselves, it is the gift of God; not as a result of works, that no one should boast."

How marvelous to know that we can do nothing to merit our salvation! Yes, Jesus has jobs for us to do, ways to use the terrific potential He has placed in each one of us. But we must never divorce the work He has for us from the necessity of sitting at His feet. And we must never make accomplishments our source of self-esteem.

The True Source Will Never Dry Up

Are you currently driving down the route of appearance, male-female relationships, motherhood or accomplishment in your search for self-esteem? Maybe, like Leah, you have tried them all. And maybe, like Leah, you are ready to make an about-face, to find the route that leads directly to the true source of self-esteem.

When did Leah turn around? When she found herself pregnant with yet another child.

Sure enough, the baby was a boy. But something changed in Leah's spirit with the birth of this little one. Genesis 29:35 says:

> And [Leah] conceived again and bore a son and said, "This time I will praise the Lord." Therefore she named him Judah. Then she stopped bearing.

This short verse tells us volumes! If you suspect Leah gave this child a name with special meaning, as she had her others, you are correct! Judah meant "praise," praise to God. "This time," she said in essence, "I will look to God for my satisfaction."

God had been trying all along to get through to Leah that attempting to find her source of self-esteem in beauty, or in her husband, or in her children or in her accomplishments, would eventually destroy her. And Leah finally woke up. She began to see that her misery was caused not by her lack of good looks. It was not solely the result of her father's insensitivity and Jacob's rejection. Neither her children nor her homemaking abilities could make her feel significant enough to ease the pain of her aching place. Leah finally realized she had to look to the God of Abraham, Isaac and Jacob, and no one else, as her source of self-esteem and joy. She needed to transfer her allegiance to the right Person.

Making Jesus the full source of our worth, dignity and importance will free us as well. If we look to anyone or anything else for affirmation of our true value, we will always be disappointed and disillusioned.

But when closeness with Jesus is an ongoing, vibrant reality in our lives, others can fall short of our expectations without damaging our emotions or self-worth. Safe in the accepting arms of Jesus, we can still love the people who disappoint us. We are free to love them with their strengths, weaknesses, accomplishments and failures, for we are not depending on them to be our source of self-esteem. We do not have to resent them to make ourselves feel better. This, in turn, will free us to love and support them in ways not possible before, thus actually enhancing these relationships.

Jesus' acceptance causes us to take shape as women because He loves *us,* not our abilities, skills or looks. The unchanging love of Jesus will begin to wash away the old patterns of self-doubt that have driven us to clamor for attention in self-defeating ways. His love will free us to risk exiting the wrong routes we have followed in our search.

When our aching places are continually being examined, touched and healed by our Lover, redemption takes on a new dimension. Not only are our sins forgiven. Not only will we be in heaven someday. There is more to redemption because now, this very minute, we are immersed in a love relationship so vital and important to both parties that nothing—not rejection, not loneliness, not circumstances in our past or present, not our fear of the future—can jar us loose from the beauty and reality of this relationship.

One more thing. As women we tend to fear change, because change in our earthly lives often signals a lessening of our importance. Our looks change, our relationships with our parents, spouses and children change, our abilities to meet others' needs may diminish. But our relationship with Jesus, our Lover, will deepen and widen into a cleansing, flowing river of intimacy, and His love for us and His role in our lives will never lessen. When we allow the Holy Spirit to plant that belief firmly in our spirits, we experience an unchanging peace in a world that is changing constantly.

We may neglect this relationship now and then, and we may have to make willful decisions every day to keep our love for Jesus alive. But we need never fear being forsaken, abandoned or rejected by our Lover. Our source of self-esteem will never dry up.

Prayer

I have considered or tried different routes to self-esteem, Lord Jesus—appearance, male-female relationships, motherhood, accomplishment. But I do not have to make these my source any longer. You alone are my strength and source, so I am free to love and accept others as You do, even if they disappoint and use me. My self-esteem lies in Your love for me, not in the opinions of others.

I rejoice in You as my complete and total source, and I am now free to praise You as Leah did. Thank You, Jesus. Amen.

6

He Uncovers Bondage That Holds You Hostage

Have you ever been introduced to someone about whom you have heard nasty rumors? What an awkward situation! You do not know quite where to look or what to think. She *seems* nice enough, but can you be sure? Do you dare offer her your friendship and trust?

Then, weeks or months later, the rumors turn out to be completely false. You learn the wonderful truth about your new acquaintance and can develop your relationship with her based on fact, not ugly fiction.

Good theology is like that. Good theology, which might be defined as sound understanding about God based on correct understanding of scriptural principles, is basic to a right relationship with Jesus. Are you beginning to recognize some faulty theological concepts about the Father, the Son or the Holy Spirit that have obstructed your rich and joyous connection with your Lover?

Even when our theology is sound, our *perceptions* of the truth about Jesus and about ourselves, and not the truth itself, often dictate the everyday actions and responses that characterize our Christian walk. Just as false rumors can color the way we view other people, so erroneous perceptions may actually hold us in bondage to attitudes and behaviors that place terrible constraints on the relaxed, loving give-and-take that should be natural in our daily interaction with Jesus.

This is why it is vital for us to allow the Holy Spirit to bring us into the reality of who Jesus is and what He has done for us. Sometimes we must let Him uncover and expose reasons we may not even be aware of that imprison us—bondages that block a satisfying relationship with our Lover.

The good news is, Jesus is aware of any and all such bondages or hindrances. And He is reaching out to you and me even before we ask Him, constantly taking the initiative, calling us by name, ready to free us from whatever obstructs. Jesus does not wait for us to understand everything perfectly, nor does He always wait for us to ask for His help. His compassion and love always go ahead of us, finding ways to touch, heal and free us. He will make sure you hear messages His Spirit can use to help you. He will put people across your path and in your life who are especially equipped to minister to your special need. Jesus' precious shed blood has paid for our sins, and that same shed blood can free us from all bondage.

Many types of bondage exist. Satan exploits all of them to keep us from connecting with Jesus in the way we were intended to do since the creation of the world. In this chapter we will examine some of the most common kinds of bondage, in an effort to help you recognize and understand their destructive patterns. In the next chapter we will discuss how you can be unshackled to follow your Lover with abandon.

First, however, let's look at a beautiful example of Jesus' power to free a woman from bondage.

Surprised by Freedom

According to Luke 13, a nameless woman "had a sickness caused by a spirit" (verse 11). The Bible is clear that not all illness comes to us in this way, but in this situation, an oppressive spirit from Satan had caused her to suffer for eighteen years. The physical manifestation of the illness was that the woman's body was "bent double," says verse 11. The verse continues that she "could not straighten up at all."

I have often pictured this woman in my mind. I have even stood up and then bent over from the waist and tried to walk. What a horrible way to get around! What a painful way to live! It would have been next to impossible for her to look up, so she spent her life looking at the ground. Because I have suffered off and on with back pain caused by degenerate discs, I know what it feels like to face the day in agony. But this woman's body ached day in and day out.

She was not consciously seeking a healing the day she encountered Jesus. It is worthwhile to note that she was in the synagogue when He approached her (see verses 10 and 12). Was she there out of habit, performing an ingrained, rote response? Did she come to the house of God because she feared what He might do if she did not follow the religious rules? Do you suppose she ever, in her wildest dreams, expected to be healed of her chronic disorder?

Perhaps, on the other hand, her relationship with the God of Abraham, Isaac and Jacob would not let her give up. Maybe her devotion to Him was such that regardless of her condition, she was committed to being in His house to pray and worship regularly. Maybe her adoration of the living God filled her spirit each Sabbath and gave her strength and courage for the new week.

Whatever the reason, Jesus found her in the synagogue. And the first thing He said to her was,

"Woman, you are freed from your sickness." And He laid His hands upon her; and immediately she was made erect again, and began glorifying God.

verses 12–13

Can you imagine her joy? No more bending over! No
more pain from the constant backache! No more looking
at the floor hour after hour! No more shame!

If the story ended here, it would be a marvelous chron-
icle of Jesus' compassion to heal. But much more than a
physical healing was involved, because the religious leaders of the day reacted with the predictability that charac-
terized their spiritual condition. Rather than rejoice over
an act of kindness from the God they professed to know
and serve, they criticized Jesus for healing this woman on
the Sabbath. I can practically hear the indignation and
scolding in their voices as they tried to embarrass Jesus by
saying to the crowd, "There are six days in which work
should be done; therefore come during them and get healed,
and not on the Sabbath day" (verse 14).

Jesus reacted according to His customary pattern, too.
He addressed His accusers with frankness and passion:

> "You hypocrites, does not each of you on the Sabbath untie
> his ox or his donkey from the stall, and lead him away to
> water him? And this woman, a daughter of Abraham as she
> is, whom Satan has bound for eighteen long years, should
> she not have been released from this bond on the Sabbath
> day?"
>
> verses 15–16

What an indictment! Jesus knew the misery of those religious leaders' spirits. He knew that their legalism and lack
of compassion revealed stony and impenetrable hearts,
hearts of different stuff altogether from the heart of God.
Jesus knew that they, like people in our midst today, were
unaware of their own bondage because they were out of
touch with the reality of who God is.

Notice, however, that after Jesus reprimanded the religious leaders, He made an observation that is central to the
character of God. He pointed out that since the woman He

had healed was a daughter of Abraham, she belonged to God. Satan had kept her bound for altogether too long, and Jesus decided it was high time she was released from this bondage. What more fitting time to do that than on the Sabbath—and, I might add, in God's house to boot?

Lessons

What can we learn from this story as we get ready to explore our own possible bondage? I see at least three wonderful insights that can help us understand our Lover's longing to free us from slavery.

1. It is good to be faithful to God no matter what is happening in our lives. Job demonstrated this principle when he voiced those well-known words, "Though He slay me, I will hope in Him" (Job 13:15). No matter what happens to me, Job was saying, I refuse to let it overcome my belief that God is in control of my situation.

The apostle Paul reinforced this theme when he instructed the Thessalonians (and, through his letter to them, instructed us), "In everything give thanks; for this is God's will for you in Christ Jesus" (1 Thessalonians 5:18). Regardless of the situations that engulf us, even threaten to overwhelm us, we can thank God that He will have an opportunity to show Himself strong on our behalf.

The woman released from her back condition was rewarded for her faithfulness to God, whether her motivation was legalism or love. She was right where Jesus wanted her to be, "voting with her feet," so to speak, and He surprised her with the wonderful gift of freedom from her bonds.

When your Lover is ready to surprise you with an answer to your dilemma, will He find you practicing faithfulness instead of infidelity? Will you be where you can hear His voice and receive His gifts of healing and freedom? Or will you be putting your faith in other things: people, money, jobs or anything else but Him to "fix" your problems? Stay ready, expectant, eagerly anticipating His action. Stay faithful and be where you can receive help. You never know when your Lover might surprise you!

2. God highly esteems those of us who belong to Him. Please do not assume that Jesus looks on you or your condition in the same way others might, even those who profess to know Him. They do not have all the facts. He does. And unlike our brothers and sisters whose "objective" evaluations are usually tainted with judgment, He mixes the facts with His everlasting mercy—His undeserved favor. He sees what is binding you. He recognizes the factors (including your sins and the sins of others) that carried you into bondage. And He longs more than anything to set you free.

What's more, it is God's character to reach out and defend us, to run interference for us when we belong to Him. Jesus wanted the bent-over woman to understand not only His compassion *for* her, but His connection *to* her. He noted her faithfulness to God, designating her a "daughter of Abraham" and thus a true daughter of God.

When you are living in a love connection with Jesus, He will never disdain you or look on you with contempt or disgust. He esteems you, honors you, longs to give you the joy and peace and self-esteem and inheritance that are yours because you are His. Paul said it clearly in Romans 8:1: "There is therefore now no condemnation for those who are in Christ Jesus." No condemnation! Gentle, loving reproof and conviction when we need it? Yes. But condemnation? No. Once we are His, He will never upbraid, blame or shame us.

3. Just as bondage affects our bodies, minds and emotions, so freedom from bondage will have an impact on our whole being. We have visualized the physical condition of the woman in

Luke 13, but she also presents a penetrating picture of someone bound emotionally, "bent over" in mind and spirit. Persons in emotional bondage cannot "look up" to see things clearly. They walk in daily humiliation and darkness.

I do not know what bondage caused this woman's illness. I do know that when Jesus recognized the binding cause and released her from it, observing that it had come from Satan and had controlled her life for a long time, she received freedom and healing for her bodily affliction.

Our bodies, minds and emotions, all created by God, are, as you know, closely knit together. What affects one, affects the other. We cannot separate them. So if your body aches, your mind and emotions will soon feel the impact. If your mind or emotions are in pain, your body will eventually hurt, too. This is why Jesus wants to set us free from all bondage. He designed us; He knows all too well the interconnectedness of mind, body and emotions.

You may be living proof of this interconnectedness. Satan may have kept you bound for who knows how long, and you have no idea of how to get free. You may not even know you are bound, for we learn to accommodate the bondage in our lives and Satan is quick to blind us to its imprisonment, its permeation of our relationships, self-esteem and intimacy with Jesus.

If you have not realized you are bound, you may not be asking consciously for freedom. But your Love, Jesus, is intimately acquainted with everything that holds you tight, and He wants to set you free.

A wonderful promise in John 8:36 says, "If therefore the Son shall make you free, you shall be free indeed." Jesus was speaking to those who would not acknowledge that He was God come in the flesh. They resisted the truth of His deity and His relationship with the Father. But to those who would believe and were willing to receive, He promised freedom.

What Bondage Is Holding You?

Just as Jesus found the woman in the synagogue, He has found you. Just as surely as His power and mercy set her free, He is working to set you free. The determination and fervor of our great Lover knows no bounds! You are His daughter, born of His Spirit. You belong to Him, and He is the Truth come to set you free. If there are bondages in your life that block your juncture with Him, He will search them out with you and destroy them.

Jesus came to "destroy the works of the devil" (1 John 3:8), and bondage is one of those works. The Son of God stands ready to look at your story with you and assure you that the fetters are being broken, the ropes being untied.

We often think of bondage as addiction to drugs or alcohol, or slavery to fleshly habits, or relationships we cannot seem to break. These are indeed bondages, and many believers are caught up in this kind of captivity. Other bondages we experience are more subtle. But whatever Satan's method of diverting our energies from our Lover, he uses bondage to discredit us—in our own eyes, in the eyes of others and before God.

How do you know if you are in some kind of bondage? Look with me in this section at three common categories of bondage. And as you do, ask the Holy Spirit to uncover anything that is holding you hostage.

1. Bondage to Past Failure

Even after we trust Jesus for salvation and enter a deeper relationship with Him by connecting with the Holy Spirit, our past failures can retain a firm and binding grip on us. Constant awareness of our past mistakes clouds the reality of His love and of His desire for us to draw close to Him. Our continuing sense of unworthiness might be heightened by memories of former blunders.

Bondage to past failure causes us to experience a vicious cycle: We love Jesus and want to experience more of His love, but we feel a nagging worry that what we have said or done in the past still stands between Him and us. Yes, we know the Scripture says we are forgiven for all our past sins, mistakes and failures, but our head knowledge does not quite break the chains that force us to listen to Satan's gleeful, unending rehearsal of "Remember when . . . ?"

Satan loves to keep us in bondage to mistakes we have made in the past. He is always ready to remind us of our failures; in fact, it is one of Satan's jobs. Remember Revelation 12:10, which tells us Satan is "the accuser of our brethren . . . who accuses them before our God day and night." Hour after hour our enemy reminds not only us, but God, of all the reasons we are still unworthy of His love. How God must tire of his nagging!

But the Scriptures also say that Jesus, our precious Lover, "always lives to make intercession" for us (Hebrews 7:25). Since intercession is prayer on behalf of others, we know that one of Jesus' activities, as He sits at the right hand of the Father, is letting Him know what we need. And often what we need is defense against the enemy's assault. *The Message* puts Hebrews 7:25 this way: "[Jesus is] always on the job to speak up for . . . [us]."

Where does Satan push your buttons? What past failures and sins still haunt you? What makes you feel unworthy of Jesus' total love and acceptance? What "if-onlys" persist, destroying your joy in the Lord?

I have talked to women who have been in bondage to heartbreaking memories of abortion. Others live with the pain and guilt of impulsive words and actions. Some women suffer physically, emotionally and mentally because they had sexual relationships outside marriage. Others know their choices of marriage partners were made for the wrong reasons, outside of God's direction. Some who have taken care of elderly parents realize that their own frustrations caused them to be unkind, even abusive.

An overwhelming number of women feel guilty over their failures at mothering. They may regret the lack of time they spent with their children. They may wonder if they made good choices in their use of discipline. They play the "what-if" game over whether they should have worked outside the home. They may feel responsible for the lifestyle of an adult child, sure that he or she is paying the price for Mom's shortcomings.

I experienced tremendous bondage over the way I mothered our first child, Jana. I never questioned my love for her, but I always held in question my ability, or lack of it, as her mother. For years I felt sadness whenever I saw a television show about an "ideal" family, especially when it portrayed great mother-daughter relationships. Each time I read a good book about family dynamics, I found myself asking Jesus to forgive me for being such an inadequate mother to Jana.

Have you ever felt guilty in your role as a mother? Satan will nurture your guilt with a vengeance! He knew all about my own feelings and deeds, and never missed an opportunity to remind me of my ineptness. He flooded my memory with vivid snapshots of parenting opportunities in which I had blown it. One came to mind more often than the rest.

When I was pregnant with our second child, Jana was less than three years old. We were living in a new neighborhood and I did not allow her to play anywhere except on our street, which offered an abundance of children and was practically traffic-free. Jana was wonderful about playing in our yard or with children from nearby houses.

But one chilly day, as I watched her from the window, I was distracted and left my post. When I came back and looked again, I could not see her. You may have gone through the same harrowing experience: the panic, the race outside to call your child's name frantically.

Jana was not far away; she had walked off with a little friend who lived on the street behind us, and ended up playing in the other child's yard. When I spotted her, I grabbed her and began telling her how she had broken the rules. I took her home, thrilled to have found her but upset with myself for not keeping better track of her. Inside I jerked off her coat and scarf, still expounding on the dangers of leaving our street. She had her lunch and went off for a nap while I continued to shudder at the thought of what could have happened.

Later that evening, as I bathed Jana, I noticed a kind of burn on her neck.

"What's this, honey?" I asked. "How did you get this mark on your neck?"

Jana's bewildered answer rang in my conscious and subconscious mind for years to come.

"That's where you hurt me, Mommy, for being bad," she explained.

I was puzzled for a moment, then realized that when I had grabbed her scarf from around her neck, I had given her a rope burn!

I swooped Jana up in my arms, wet as she was, explaining desperately that I had not hurt her on purpose. I held her close and told her over and over how sorry I was.

Jana does not remember that incident, at least not consciously, but it activated guilt in me for years. I felt responsible for every act of rebellion in her teen years. I know now she was rebelling at the right age and in the protection of a place where she was loved. But I always felt like a failure in our relationship, certain that whatever problems Jana had were the direct result of my insensitive mothering. (And believe me, the scarf incident was not the worst of my sins!) I was in bondage to my own feelings of guilt and unworthiness, and no matter how often I asked Jesus to forgive me, the condemnation remained.

Is Jesus speaking to you? Are you, too, haunted by past failures? Keep reading. Do not lose hope. Our Redeemer God promises to "make up to you for the years that the swarming locust has eaten" (Joel 2:25).

2. Bondage to Circumstances

A myriad of circumstances in our lives can rob us of our joy, peace and freedom if we allow them to. Perhaps your own illness, or that of a loved one, keeps you at home, unable to enjoy life's pleasures. Maybe you have a disabled or seriously ill child. Why you? Why your loved one? And why are there no answers to the hourly pleas you send heavenward for healing—or for just a bit of respite from the suffering and confinement that make up your days?

Other circumstances may be creating "dis-ease" in your life. Perhaps a significant person with whom you interact—a relative, a co-worker, even a fellow church member—is selfishly manipulative, despite all your efforts to break free. Perhaps your job or church setting is unfulfilling or stifling. Perhaps unemployment threatens to destroy the financial security you have worked so hard to build.

Or maybe, like my friend Angie, who married in spite of her parents' strong disapproval, you feel there is no "fix" for your circumstances. Your parents were right: Your husband's background and lifestyle *are* vastly different from yours. When the first blush of romance wore off, you found out you disagree on almost everything that is important to you. But you chose him, knowingly or unknowingly letting yourself in for the relationship and the accompanying events that now threaten to devour your joy in life, your very spirit. How will you survive the next thirty or forty years?

You think of other women in unhappy marriages as well, women whose parents have refused to help them sort out their situations. "You made your bed," they say unfeelingly. "Now lie in it."

"Maybe that's the way Jesus feels about me," you say. "Why should He rescue me when the whole mess is of my own making?"

Take heart. Jesus cares about each circumstance of our lives. He knows when illness, Satan, other people or the consequences of our own decisions victimize us—and He longs to defend us and help us gain His victory. Read on for one more category of bondage; then we will move on to some solutions.

3. Bondage to Unforgiveness

Bondage to past failures and circumstances is devastatingly common, but one poisonous, devious bondage runs rampant throughout the Body of Christ. What is it? The bondage to unforgiveness, the inability or unwillingness to forgive others, practiced by the very people who have received the unqualified, undeserved mercy and forgiveness of God. Because unforgiveness is the underlying bondage of many people, and because it is so opposed to the character of our Lover, I try to include something about the importance of forgiveness in almost every message I give, and I consider it of grave importance for us to consider now. This single bondage is the granddaddy of many a heartache, many a broken relationship and much diminished fellowship and intimacy with Jesus.

Once bondage to unforgiveness takes effect, its enslavement motivates every area of our beings—body, mind and spirit. What does the Bible say about unforgiveness?

God makes it abundantly clear in His Word that once we enter the covenant of His unmerited grace and forgiveness, He expects us to become forgivers, too. "Be kind to one another, tender-hearted, forgiving each other, just as God in Christ also has forgiven you." That command from Ephesians 4:32 leaves no room for whim or debate. God gave the supreme example in His own forgiveness of our sins, and in the forgiveness Jesus extended continually while here on earth.

The definitive New Testament discussion about God's expectations in this area is found in Matthew 18, where we find Jesus' parable about a man who owed an enormous debt. He could not pay this obligation and begged his master for more time. "Have patience with me," he pleaded, "and I will repay you everything" (verse 26).

Surprisingly, Jesus told His disciples that "the lord of that slave felt compassion and released him and forgave the debt" (verse 27). The debtor was off the hook. He would not be thrown into prison; he would not have to spend restless nights wondering where he would come up with the money. He was free of it all because of the sheer mercy of his master. He was one happy man!

The story does not end here, of course. Jesus went on to say that this same man, now debt-free, "went out and found one of his fellow-slaves who owed him a hundred denarii; and he seized him and began to choke him, saying, 'Pay back what you owe'" (verse 28). The sum owed the forgiven man, about eighteen cents in silver, was nothing like the one he himself had owed—more than ten million dollars. But when the debtor begged, "Have patience with me and I will repay you" (verse 29), the debt-free man refused. He demanded payment immediately and, when the poor man could not comply, had him thrown into prison.

Who would act so unkindly after being shown such grace? You would think this man would be so filled with gratitude for his own situation, so full of joy over the cancellation of his debt, that he would gladly show mercy and dismiss this lesser debt.

Jesus' point, of course, was to make the connection between the forgiven, freed but ungrateful debtor and us when we are unwilling to forgive others. God will not tolerate such behavior, and Jesus drove home the lesson by finishing the story. The exacting debtor's unforgiving behavior was reported to his master who, furious at his lack of compassion, handed him over to the torturers until he paid every dime of his debt.

"So shall My heavenly Father also do to you," Jesus concluded, "if each of you does not forgive his brother from your heart" (verse 35).

What a wake-up call! After all, most of us pray with regularity that part of the Lord's Prayer: "Forgive us our debts, as we forgive our debtors" (see Matthew 6:12). But do we really mean it? We want and expect God to forgive us, but I doubt we want His forgiveness to be extended to us in the same mingy way we often dole it out! We want God to be far swifter and far more merciful than we are.

Our Lover is tender yet firm with us. He knows it is in the way we handle offenses that God often reveals our understanding of His mercy and grace. The more we comprehend and accept His forgiveness of us, the more we will be able to forgive others. And the converse is true: If we are not able to show mercy to those who come against us, there is good reason to believe we have never entered God's grace with "arms-wide-open" abandon. We have not understood our own forgiveness.

What Is Forgiveness?

At this point you may be wondering just what forgiveness is.

1. Forgiveness is a willful act of obedience to God, not an emotion. Jesus insists that we become forgivers. He commands it. But He really could not do so if forgiveness were an emotion, because God, who made us, knows that feelings cannot be commanded.

No, forgiveness is not a feeling. It springs instead from our wills. And our God-given free wills—our decision-making capabilities and not our emotions—are best equipped to help us choose to forgive. On what do we base that choice? Not on the upheaval an offense (and offender) have caused us, but on our desire to obey and please our Lover.

When we choose to forgive, we free God to begin healing our emotions. Unfortunately, most people try to turn this principle around. They cry out to Jesus to heal the pain, and agree in their hearts to forgive the offender once the pain is gone.

Forgiveness does not and cannot work that way. We must first forgive out of love and obedience to Jesus (not necessarily, at this point, the offender). Then we can rest in His grace as our emotions are bathed in His healing balm. Some dear Christian brother or sister put it best: "Feelings *follow* forgiveness."

2. Forgiveness is giving up our right to be right! This means we will not hold unforgiveness in our hearts simply because we are right in a given situation and the other person is wrong. I have counseled people who have been so hurt by others that I know they are sane only by the grace of God. There is no doubt they were wronged or that the offenses were hideous and ungodly.

But our rightness in a situation is no license to hold a grudge or refuse to forgive. The minute we receive the full grace of God through the blood of Jesus for ourselves personally, we give up the right to be right.

When Jesus hung on that cross, He was innocent. He had a right, by today's standards, to hate those who were hurting Him. As God He had a right to call legions of angels to come to His rescue, and a right to destroy the offenders. But Jesus gave up all these rights so He could buy our pardon and secure forgiveness for our sin.

We, too, are called to give up the right to hold resentment and bitterness, even when we are innocent victims.

One woman approached me during a conference.

"I want you to listen to my story," she began, "and still tell me I have no right to feel the way I do!"

She went on to relate the sad story of how she had watched over her aging mother until her death. She was the primary caregiver, even though she had brothers and sisters in the area. None of them, in her opinion, was interested in helping her. She put her own life on hold so she could devote time and energy to the mother she loved dearly.

"I don't regret a single minute of the time I gave Mother," she insisted. "She knew how much I loved her."

I listened with interest, wondering what this woman's problem with unforgiveness might be, but suspecting I already knew the answer.

Sure enough, she finally snapped, "And now that Mother is gone, they all want to share in her estate! They did nothing to help me when she was alive, but now they want to make sure they are not left out of her will."

I hear many similar stories, each with a different scenario, players, hurts and offenses, but all with the same sense of injustice. This woman loved her mother and thought she was caring for her without bitterness. But she resented those who were not helping, and now that the mother was gone, those resentments had surfaced with incredible strength.

"Are you a believer?" I asked her.

"Yes," she replied, "I am."

So I talked about her relationship with Jesus, about her love for Him and His for her. I reminded her of His command to forgive, and about how our response to His command is tied to our own acceptance of His forgiveness for us.

"But caring for my mother was so lonely," the woman sobbed. "I needed my siblings' help, but I needed their encouragement and praise, too. They were never there for me. They had no idea how it hurt to face losing Mother— and to give up my normal life. They failed me!"

Hurt and angry, she wanted someone to pay.

"What is your relationship with your family members now?" I asked.

"I'm protesting the will because Mother left us all equal shares in her inheritance," she answered. "I feel my siblings don't deserve this." Then she confessed, "They're not speaking to me."

"Is it worth all this for you to be right?" I asked.

She cried some more. Finally she looked up at me with what actually resembled a smile. "Would you pray with me and help me choose to forgive?"

The Holy Spirit had helped this woman decide to forgive and surrender the resentment she thought she had the right to hold. I am sure He was working in her heart long before she talked to me. Forgiving those who had let her down, she let go of her rights that day and was set free from a bondage that could have kept her prisoner the rest of her life. True to His nature, her Lover made sure she was at the right place at the right time to hear, understand, receive and act.

One more principle will help us to understand what forgiveness is.

3. *Forgiveness is a choice we must practice daily.* You may be in a situation or relationship in which you need to practice forgiveness hour by hour!* For most of us forgiveness must be an ongoing choice. We do not come to this fountain once; we live there! We have to make decisions every single day to forgive, to let go of resentment. And the more we practice forgiveness, the more resolved we are to being forgivers. Choosing forgiveness is indeed freeing!

My friend Karen was a beautiful woman with a gentle countenance and charming smile. Elegant in appearance, she was in her mid-forties, married, with children. She and her family were well loved and respected in the church and community. So the first time Karen called for an appoint-

---

*I am not talking here about submitting to an abusive situation. If you are in physical danger or subjected to constant emotional abuse, you will need, first of all, to choose to get to a place of safety. Then you can deal with forgiveness.

ment, I wondered what she could possibly want. Everything seemed to be going right for her. (We never know from looking at others the anguish they may be experiencing.) But Karen had a need she had never shared with anyone.

"I am getting older every day, Jan," she began, "and my looks are all I have going for me."

And so the story unfolded. Karen had grown up with a mother and father who had remained married and were still alive. She considered her father a good parent. He had taken an interest in her and her sister and worked hard for his family. But Karen's father had made a remark, apparently quite often, that rang in her memory.

"Honey," he would say, "your sister, Emily, is the one with the brains. You're the one with the looks. They're what you have going for you."

Over and over this thought was reinforced as she related to her dad.

"But Karen," I said, "you're a Christian now. You know you consist of much more than your looks."

She knew. She was a strong believer and had a love relationship with Jesus. She had all kinds of spiritual truths tucked deep in her spirit. But she could not seem to let go of this distorted view of herself, especially since it had been imparted by someone she loved and trusted.

So each new wrinkle brought fear to Karen's spirit. Each gray hair made her feel she was losing the one thing of value she possessed, her good looks.

Karen and I counseled together over a long time, and I found that many people besides her father had reinforced the lie that had shaped her life. Karen decided to forgive them all. This was necessary not to place blame, but to free her from the bondage of her father's words and the agreement of others.

As Karen began to forgive, I saw new changes in her almost weekly. How delightful it was to see her splash in her Lover's fountain of forgiveness and self-esteem by making willful choices to forgive, and releasing the false concepts of herself to Him!

I knew Karen was making forgiveness a principle she practiced daily when I saw her handle another hurtful situation. She called one day excited because, after looking for a part-time job, she had been asked to become the new church secretary. We made a date for lunch so I could hear all about it.

We arrived at the restaurant and placed our orders before I was finally able to say, "Tell me about your new job!"

Karen never skipped a beat.

"As it turns out," she said, "I won't have that job after all."

"I thought it was a done deal."

"It was. But our pastor's sister-in-law moved to town and he decided to give her the job instead."

What could I say?

"How do you feel about this?" I asked finally.

"Oh, Jan," she responded, "you're the one who told me I have to live in the fountain of forgiveness! I love my pastor and my church too much to allow this to come between us. I've chosen to forgive."

Karen had learned she could not be a forgiver just once or twice, but daily, and regardless of the injustice. She made sure that bitterness did not take root in her spirit. She had seen the results already of being a forgiver, and she saw the need to practice it yet again in this new situation.

We are never closer to the heart of our Lover than when we walk each day in the practice of forgiveness.

Forgiveness Is Hard

Neither of Karen's situations was easy to handle. It might appear that she moved into forgiveness more easily regarding her job loss than she did in relationship to her father's life-shaping words. But that was only because she had learned how to practice the principle.

Forgiveness is hard for at least two reasons. First, it is not natural. When someone hurts or offends us or someone we love, we automatically rise up to defend, protect and vindicate at all costs. This is an automatic human response. In commanding forgiveness, God asks us to do the unnatural, the supernatural. Why? Because He loves, He embraces, He values forgiveness. When we practice forgiveness, we bring pleasure to Him, increasing our intimacy.

Our Lover also knows that failing to forgive will put us in bondage to the thing that was said or done to us. The offense will control us, preventing us from enjoying our relationship with Him to the fullest extent. So we will benefit by looking at forgiveness from every angle, ridding ourselves of misconceptions about it and embracing our Lover's command.

There is a second reason forgiveness is hard: We are often afraid that to forgive puts us in the position of looking weak.

I hear women say frequently that if they were to forgive the one who hurt them, they would be letting that person off the hook, condoning what was said or done or acting like a doormat.

"I can't forgive," goes this line of reasoning. "It hurts too much, and besides, they were wrong. If I forgive, they will never know how wrong they were and how much they hurt me." Or, "I can't forgive until he apologizes and admits he was wrong."

Have you ever felt this way? I have. But again, these are misconceptions, wrong attitudes about forgiveness.

Failing to forgive does not change anyone else, but it will destroy you. Unforgiveness causes loss of sleep, bitterness and tremendous tension in our lives. When we fail to resolve a hurtful situation through forgiveness, we cannot let go of what was said or done, nor can we shoo Satan away whenever he brings it to mind. With his all-too-willing help, we replay it over and over in our minds, and if we can get someone to listen to us, we share the offense in the hopes that he or she will affirm our right to feel the way we do and to hang onto the resentment. We may think we are free of our resentment as time goes on, because we do not think of it as often. But unless we have dealt with it through forgiveness, we have only pushed it to a subconscious level, where its venom still controls our lives.

I hope you are beginning to see the damage unforgiveness wreaks in the lives of everyone involved. Perhaps you have tried to break this bondage, only to find yourself in chains again. You think you have forgiven someone, but his or her offense keeps tripping you up. Or maybe you know you have not forgiven someone, but wonder exactly how to go about it for keeps. Chapter 7 will help us to explore those dilemmas.

Once You Have Discovered the Problem . . .

Has Jesus put His finger on some bondage that is keeping you from living life as He meant you to live it? Has He uncovered a past failure, a circumstance or an instance of unforgiveness in your life from which you need to shake free? If so, take hold of His strong, liberating hand and deal with the problem now. You have a God-given opportunity for freedom; why go back to prison?

Taking Jesus' outstretched hand is the first step in ridding yourself of bondage. What else do you need to do in order for Jesus to set you free? If some bondage has affected you, how do you counteract those effects? Read on for some biblical answers, and allow your Lover to work mightily in your life.

Prayer

Gracious Lover, I have been bent over long enough. Please uncover any bondage that is keeping me from a fuller, warmer, deeper relationship with You and with others. Search out every hindrance, until each one bows down to Your name and authority. In Your strong name I ask, Amen.

7

He Frees You from Bondage

Psychologists and social behaviorists have come up with no magic formula for freeing people from the different kinds of bondage we have discussed that compares in any way to the simple patterns offered in God's Word. I have applied these patterns in my own life, cooperating with Jesus to break out of imprisonment to past failure, to circumstances and to unforgiveness.

You can follow the same biblical patterns to find freedom and send Satan packing.

Letting Your Lover Help You Break Free

1. From Bondage to Past Failures

In order to allow Jesus to set me free from bondage to past failures as a mother, I had to talk to Jesus about it one last time. There would be no repeat of this conversation, because in His eyes it was settled. I needed to see it as settled, too. This one last conversation included the following interchanges:

1. *I asked forgiveness for missing the mark, for falling short of the biblical mandates.* I had to come to terms with

123

the fact that I was not (and still am not) a perfect mother. Our heavenly Father is the only perfect Parent. I wish I had done many things differently and that I had known back then how to give Jesus full reign in my life. But I cannot change how things were.

2. *I told Jesus I would trust Him for His forgiveness and determine to live in His forgiveness.* It is our inability to trust His forgiveness as real, and to live every day in the state of being forgiven, that keeps us in prison. Until we take ownership of His grace (unmerited favor) to cover our past mistakes, as He wants us to, they will continue to hold us hostage.

3. *I released my past failures to the blood of Jesus once and for all*—every failed deed, every failed attitude, every hurtful word. I had to purpose in my heart that these were gone—as indeed they are, according to God's Word. The prophet Micah tells us our sins are "cast . . . into the depths of the sea" (7:19). Alexander Cruden remarked in his *Unabridged Concordance* that "what is cast into the depth of the sea is ordinarily accounted as lost, we have no expectation of finding it any more; so to cast sins into the depth of the sea imports the full and free pardon of them." My failures were no longer mine. I had lost power over them, so they lost their power over me.

4. Finally (and this is where many of us experience disappointment), although I felt no different after this last conversation with Jesus about these particular sins, *I continued to reaffirm my release from bondage to past failures and cling to the fact of His promise.* Slowly I began to sense freedom.

2. From Bondage to Circumstances

Your Lover knows and aches over the circumstances that seem more than you can bear. It does not matter whether they originated in the sins of others or whether you have victimized yourself by making bad choices. Jesus does not need you to play the blame game or grovel in self-deprecation. A simple turning of your heart toward Him in admission of need or repentance is enough to open the floodgates of His tender yet powerful deliverance. No scolding. He asks just one question: *Do you want things to change badly enough to cooperate with Me?*

If your answer is yes, He goes to work, first on you, then through you, on the circumstances. The following clues will help you know how to cooperate with Him.

Choosing to Be Content

The first clue to cooperating with God to gain victory over your bondage to circumstances comes from the apostle Paul, who wrote, "I have learned to be content in whatever circumstances I am" (Philippians 4:11). Paul was suggesting that anyone can manage to be content in whatever situation she finds herself. But how?

By realizing that the principle of living by faith and not by sight is tested in the crucible of circumstances. This means we must choose to stay in constant touch with our Lover, clinging to His promises and allowing Him to transform us when our circumstances seem overwhelming. He must be our abiding Source, providing all the grace we need to triumph in each situation, whether or not it looks as if it will ever change. Jesus must be our strength, the One who brings delight and peace to our hearts.

But we will experience His marvelous strength, joy and power to transform us only if we choose to do so. Paul said he had to learn to be content; contentment did not come without deliberate effort on his part to retrain his thinking. So long as we pout, whine, make demands of God or others, or seek escape through television, substance abuse or some other means, our circumstances will continue to control us. But when we let go of ungodly and ineffective alternatives, our Lover can begin to set us free.

Choosing to Trust Jesus

The second clue for cooperating with God involves trusting Jesus, by an act of your will, in all the events of your life. Once you do, you will believe He is working in ways you do not know and accomplishing His purposes in you, no matter what appears to be happening on the surface.

It is an ever-enlightening, ever-enriching cycle. The reality of His active intervention in our lives, which will become more and more obvious as we trust Him more deeply, will help us release each new circumstance and development to His daily care, amazing grace and wonder-working power. And in the process we will discover a contentment we never imagined possible—a contentment that comes not from the circumstances themselves, but from our relationship with the Lover who is in control of the circumstances.

3. From Bondage to Unforgiveness

You can cooperate with your Lover to break free from unforgiveness by asking yourself, first of all, "Whom do I need to forgive?"

If one person and his or her offense looms large in your mind, this may seem a silly question. But the bondage to unforgiveness is subtle. It is easy, for instance, to be deceived into considering forgiveness necessary only in the case of enormous offenses, or assuming that unforgiveness is not a problem *we* struggle with. Yet God says we are to cancel all debts, large or small. What about the Little League coach who seldom lets your child play? Or the person at church who is always complaining? How about the boss who never seems to appreciate anything you do and has passed you over for promotions? Remember the teacher who was unfair and the pastor who let you down?

Our lives are filled with people to forgive. And we have not even mentioned the offenses so horrible they defy explanation, the ones that shattered our lives and left us reeling from shock!

Sometimes the person we need to forgive is no longer alive, or someone we have lost touch with, or someone who hurt us so long ago that the memory pops up only now and again, but still brings anger and resentment. The Holy Spirit can help us deal with these offenses, too.

Or perhaps the one you need to forgive is yourself. You may be stuck in unforgiveness because you disappointed yourself in such a way that your thoughts about yourself are demeaning and full of self-hatred. Perhaps you believe Jesus feels the same way. I must stress that He does not! He encourages you to forgive yourself as surely as He encourages you to forgive others. Holding an offense against yourself is as binding as holding it against another and His command to forgive includes self. If you don't, it clouds your relationship with your Lover, keeps Him at a distance and keeps you enslaved.

One other thought about forgiving self. If we do *not* do this, we run the risk of trying subtly to expiate our own sins. We feel somehow that by holding onto the unforgiveness, we are atoning for our sin. This is dangerous and can bring on self-pity as a result. Forgiving self is also practicing obedience to the Lord, and it closes the door to Satan's further destruction. We *cannot* atone for our sin by holding onto the guilt.

What? Forgive God?

Here is more food for thought: Some people harbor deep anger and resentment against God. They may not verbalize it, but it is there.

"But God never sins," you say. "How blasphemous to think of forgiving God!"

No, God never sins, but sometimes, after all is said and done, only God could have changed a situation and made things turn out differently, and He did not. Where was the God who claims to be our rescuer, our deliverer? Why did He allow such suffering?

When we perceive a situation in this way, our disappointment and grief may turn inward, planting a seed of doubt in our spirits that God is not altogether good after all. Without knowing it, we begin to resent Him.

Recently a young woman who had lost a child to cancer said to me, "I'm mad at God and He knows it. I am angry with Him but I still love Him."

My heart went out to her. She reminded me of Mary and Martha, special friends of Jesus who were angry at Him after they lost their brother to death, because He could have come to the rescue and did not.

This modern-day "Mary" knew that only God could have saved her child. Inexplicably, He did not. His seeming disinterest had left her hurt and confused. Whom could she blame? Only God. She could not reconcile the way she had been treated by her Lover. She had to face her own feelings and reevaluate her concepts of God. She needed to talk it out with her Lover and forgive Him for not doing what she begged Him to.

How Do You Forgive?

I hope by now you are thinking, *I'm ready to choose forgiveness. I want to be free of this bondage.*

How can you begin? Here are two straightforward steps to take.

1. Acknowledge the offense and the pain it has caused you. You may have been replaying a tape over and over and feel no need to acknowledge what is hurting you. But now, once and for all, in the presence of Jesus, voice the offense. It may help to do so out loud.

Acknowledging the offense involves admitting you were the victim of someone else's free will. He or she used that free will to hurt you in word or deed, or both. Talk to your Lover about the offense. Tell Him how it hurt you, how it still hurts and binds you. Let Him cry with you as you remember the pain. Let Him hold you close in His arms. Jesus does not take lightly the deeds of others against us, His chosen ones. He will not override the free will of the offender, but you need to know that He was there in the shadows all the time, weeping with you and going before you with a plan for your deliverance and healing. Jesus knows every look of disapproval, every damaging word, every wound, every act of violence or betrayal. You can trust your Lover to understand.

2. Decide to forgive, refusing to let your emotions or distress stand in the way. It may help to recall the sense of joy and appreciation you felt when you first knew your own sins had been forgiven.

Go back in your mind to Calvary. Gaze into the face of Jesus. Look at His hands and feet, pierced through for your sin. See His eyes of compassion as He dies there in your place. Visualize Him taking your own sin onto His shoulders. See the agony it causes and the love with which He bears it. The cost of your forgiveness is all paid with His grace and mercy.

Merit is not the foundation on which we were forgiven by Jesus, and it cannot be the foundation on which we forgive. You and I did not deserve to have our sins canceled. If we wait until people deserve our forgiveness, we may wait a lifetime. Our Lover did not wait until we deserved His favor and love; He gave it while we were undeserving.

Now remember the parable from Matthew 18. Do not be foolish enough to think you can repay the debt of your sin to Jesus if only He gives you enough time! You and I can never repay Him, for the debt of our sin is impossible for us to pay. We can never make it up to Him or even the score.

God's forgiveness, on the other hand, is fathomless. We cannot grasp its full splendor with our finite minds. Yet it is real, and we can step into His grace with awe and gratitude beyond measure. All He asks in return is that we enter a life of forgiveness and grace ourselves, extending to others the mercy He has extended to us.

One caution: We have the mistaken notion that since it is our own decision to forgive, we can simply decide not to do it. End of discussion. Yes, we can decide not to forgive, but if we do so, we must be willing to live with the bondage and its consequences. There are many consequences, as we have seen, but the most devastating is the loss of fellowship with the One who loves us most, our Lover, Jesus. Unforgiveness creates a chasm between us. Our decision to forgive bridges the gap and sets us free.

It is your decision. Will you decide to forgive?

Why Does My "Freedom" Never Last?

"I have tried all these biblical patterns for breaking free from bondage, Jan," you may be saying. "I have traveled each route. Do you know how many times I have admitted my need for God's liberation? Do you know how often I have tried to trust Him in the midst of my depressing circumstances? Do you know how hard I have tried to forgive the one who damaged my reputation? Do you know how many times I've 'released' my sins to the depths of God's sea of forgiveness, only to find my lap full of their soggy stickiness?"

Yes, I do know, because I have walked that road, too. And the reasons Satan's chains hold us, despite our following God's patterns, are:

1. His uncanny persistence in bringing our pasts back to mind in full Technicolor;
2. Our inability to recognize his tactics;
3. Our lack of assertiveness in refusing, rejecting and rebuffing his attempts to recapture us.

One minute we know in our heads we are free from bondage. The next minute we are wallowing once again in despair. How can we defang Satan's accusations?

Here is a practical, everyday strategy that works:

- *Be resolute in receiving freedom from your bondage.* Once the ropes have been untied, refuse, on a daily basis, to allow them to be tied again. When Satan pours on the guilt, begin to thank the Lord that you are forgiven and all this has been settled. Let go of the thought that brings condemnation and do not nurse it. Tell Satan firmly that "there is . . . no condemnation for those who are in Christ Jesus" (Romans 8:1) and command him in Jesus' name to leave you alone.

  Do this over and over until you begin to experience what the Bible calls "the renewing of your mind" (Romans 12:2) in this area. Do it until (concerning these mistakes and others) you are walking freely in the victory Jesus won for you at Calvary.
- *Ask your Lover to point out ways this bondage has affected your life, your opinion of yourself, of Him and of others.* Agree to let Him continue to point out ways as you walk out your newfound freedom. Be willing to form new thought patterns and new actions to accompany them.
- *Expect this new freedom to change you—and when it does, cooperate.* When I finally dealt with the bondage to past failure in my own life, and placed all Satan's condemnation for the last time beneath the blood of Jesus, I also asked Jana to forgive me for my failures

as her mother. She was no longer a little girl, but I believe it was from that day forward that our relationship took a beautiful turn. I began to relate to her differently, as she did to me. Today she is a precious young Christian woman with whom I have a treasured friendship.

I have often wondered if the woman in Luke 13 was bent over from all the accusations of Satan over her past failures. Perhaps the spirit that crippled her body was the spirit of self-condemnation. Whatever it was, she was set free by Jesus, for no spirit or bondage can withstand His name and power—not even the one that is harassing you!

Jesus Wants to Free You Completely!

Satan has so many other prisons in which he loves to contain us that we cannot possibly discuss all of them: prisons of attitudes like self-pity and criticism (of ourselves or others), prisons of unconfessed sin, prisons of fear or worry, prisons of habits that ruin our health and undermine our self-respect.

The story in Luke 13 is not clear regarding which kind of captivity gripped the woman Jesus met in the synagogue. But the good news is, He freed her completely!

Jesus is anxious to free you, too. Ask Him if there are bondages in your life that hinder your intimacy with Him. Then listen. Remember, He has been trying to free you for a long time. He sees what these bondages are doing to your mind, body and spirit. Remember, too, that His tenderness has brought you to a point of decision. Will you appropriate His freeing power?

Refuse to go back to your old imprisonment. Talk to Jesus right now. Lean back in His arms of love and hear Him whisper to your spirit, *You have been bound long enough. Daughter of mine, be free!*

Our Lover wants not only to shake us free from bondage, but to comfort us and weep with us in the big and little sorrows of our lives. So in the next chapter we will glimpse a seldom-mentioned facet of His personality: His sensitivity to our grief and pain.

Prayer

Jesus, You are so good to free me from every bondage that keeps me from living in the liberating victory Your passion bought for me. Please free me from judgment, criticism, fear and self-pity. Show me the people I need to forgive, and then give me grace to obey Your command. Help me remember that I stand forgiven by Your grace and that I must become a forgiver.

I have been bent over long enough, dear Savior, and I accept the release You offer me as Your cherished daughter. In Your freeing name I pray, Amen.

8

He Teaches You to Sit at His Feet

We live in a society that is "do-oriented." All too often (as I mentioned in chapter 5), men and women get caught up in wrapping their self-esteem around their accomplishments. Think about it: How often does a new acquaintance ask you who you *are?* If your experience is at all like mine, the answer to that question is "Rarely, if ever!" Rather, "What do you do?" is the most frequent query.

Furthermore, our culture has developed popular (and sometimes politically correct) value judgments or determinations about what kinds of "doing" are better, or more important, than others. Often the only accomplishments that receive validation are the visible, tangible ones—especially if those accomplishments produce money or status or power. The "doing" that contributes to the mind, heart or spirit of a person or community all too often goes unrecognized and unappreciated.

One consequence of this emphasis on doing has been a huge corresponding move toward setting priorities. Christians and non-Christians alike teach and attend conferences, seminars and workshops, and write and read books and articles *ad infinitum* on the matter of deciding what should take first—or second or third—priority in a person's life. Should it be God? The workplace? What about the family? One's country? And what about good old Number One?

When it comes to setting priorities, our heavenly Lover has an agenda that supersedes all others. According to the world's standards, it breaks every "get-ahead-at-all-costs," time-management, cost-efficiency, psychological and sociological rule. If we want to develop and maintain a long-lasting, challenging, growing relationship with Jesus, we need to find out what is important to Him. On what does He long to have us stamp *Top Priority* in our everyday lives?

Our Lover's Top Priority

The story of Jesus' friendship with Mary, Martha and Lazarus—and, in particular, an incident that happened during one of their visits—sheds enormous light on the question of priorities. (See Luke 10:38–42 for the biblical account.)

Jesus had a special relationship with this family. Their home in Bethany was a place our Lord came to rest, fellowship and be renewed. On this particular day Martha welcomed Him into their home and apparently began to fix an elaborate meal. Mary, on the other hand, seated herself at Jesus' feet and began to listen, absorbed in what He had to say.

Then Martha became annoyed that Mary was not moving an inch toward the kitchen to help.

"Lord," she asked boldly, "do You not care that my sister has left me to do all the serving alone? Then tell her to help me" (Luke 10:40).

I am sure Martha thought that Jesus was simply not aware of the situation, that He did not realize Mary was shirking her duty. What a shock it must have been when Jesus did not reprimand her sister, but told Martha that she, not Mary, had made a choice less than pleasing to Him.

The Bible does not say how Martha reacted. I hope she stopped fussing with preparations and came out to sit at His feet along with Mary.

Later in Jesus' ministry, however, we find Martha still in the kitchen as her sister took yet another opportunity to lavish her love on their wonderful Friend (see John 12:1–3). Apparently her long-standing pattern of active self-sufficiency was difficult to break.

Exactly what was Jesus trying to tell these women about His agenda, about what He loved? And what message does our Lover's story hold for us?

The message is this: *Jesus wants us to make sitting at His feet in order to know Him intimately our top priority in life.* Building this one-on-one relationship must be our willing, number-one choice.

What Jesus Was Not *Saying*

Before we dive into the implications of our Lover's command, we need to look at what Jesus was *not* saying in this passage. Three pervasive misconceptions may have hindered Martha from receiving His emphasis on priorities, and they hinder us today. What are they?

First of all, Jesus was not saying in this passage that one human temperament is better than another, spiritually or in any other way. I do not believe Jesus sees energetic women with go-getter personalities as less acceptable than women who are docile and laid back. He understands all facets of all personality types. (After all, He created them!)

I have heard some women declare, "I was born a Martha and there's no changing me." In terms of personality type, they may be correct. But Jesus was not discussing personality types. He was (and is) interested in whether getting to know Him eagerly, hungrily, is a top priority in your life and mine.

Second, Jesus was not telling Mary, Martha or us that accomplishments and service to others are bad choices. He was saying that He wants our doing for Him to grow out of the passion and love that fill us when we sit at His feet.

His goal is for us to know Him. When we do, the overflow of our love will result in effective service to Him. (We will examine this concept in more depth later in this chapter.)

Third, I am sure Mary was not in the habit of allowing Martha to do all the work in their home; and Jesus was downgrading neither Martha's abilities and interests nor the importance of cooperation. In fact, as the Bible tells us, Jesus frequently sampled and enjoyed Martha's hospitality; and I am sure He complimented her capability on occasion. But on this particular day He perceived that she was choosing her own interests over His.

Mary somehow sensed that this day and this visit were out of the ordinary—perhaps more than some of Jesus' other visits. The Master wanted to talk with them. And Mary, caught up in adoring wonder, saw that sitting at His feet and consuming His words and friendship were far more important than the dinner menu and table settings. She was experiencing the closeness she longed for, the closeness Jesus desired to have with her. Nothing took priority over this intimacy.

A Contemporary Model

Some years ago Candy, a young woman in my home church, taught me much about the relative importance of relationship as opposed to doing. Candy and her husband, who had four children of their own, felt led by the Lord to take in foster children, too. At any given time, their home included two to five foster youngsters of varying ages. Seeing the whole family at church each Sunday made many of us wonder where Candy got the strength to take care of so many and do it so well. Even with her husband's love and support, we knew that tons of dishes, diapers and laundry must have claimed nearly every minute, leaving little time for her.

One morning when I went to visit Candy, I saw a picture that will always linger in my memory. There she was, straddle-legged in the middle of the floor, playing with her brood. Joy and affection so filled the room that all I wanted to do was sit, observe and soak in it.

Then I looked at the house. Milk jugs, cereal boxes and breakfast dishes still sat on the table. Stacks of unfolded laundry filled one corner; toys and games were scattered everywhere. But the giggles and delight of those children told me that undone chores were not Candy's priority at the moment. She was choosing to pour love and affirmation into her little ones while she could. And as she shared the love of Jesus by singing Scripture songs and giving of herself to someone else's children, she was teaching her own offspring lessons in compassion.

It was obvious that Jesus had whispered to her about these things, letting her know they took precedence over how her house looked. For this season in her life, Candy had chosen the better part.

What Does It Mean to Sit at the Feet of Jesus?

How often we get distracted by the pull of the world and fail to choose the better part: making an intimate relationship with Jesus our top priority.

"But I don't have time to sit at His feet," you may be saying. "Mary had no Day-Timer to keep up with, no husband or children that we know of, no church or community activities demanding her attention. She had all the time in the world."

No one has time. No one. It is a matter of priority, a question of the will. We must purpose to set time apart with our Lover in an attitude of adoration, giving Him our undivided attention. I hear women pray, "Lord, I need to sit at Your feet. Give me grace and strength to do it." Jesus has already done that! Our prayer should be, "Jesus, mold my will that I *choose* to sit at Your feet."

Part of maturing in the Lord is learning to neglect some good things in order to do things that are better. We make choices each day as to how we will spend our time. Intimacy with our Lover should be our natural desire as we walk with Him. Once we make this choice by an act of the will and taste its goodness, we will want to arrange our lives to come to that place of fellowship regularly and frequently.

As we journey along with our Lover, we will discover that He is jealous. He does not want us to fit Him into our agenda; He wants us to make Him our whole agenda, and fit everything else around that commitment! The amount of time we spend at His feet is not necessarily the point (although our allocations of time say much about what we deem important). But Jesus is looking at our priorities and at the quality of our intimacy with Him. If all our doing robs us of the time we need for personal relationship with Him and growing in His love, we need to take stock and see what we can put aside in our lives in order to place intimacy with our Lover at the top of the list.

Psalm 37:4 says, "Delight yourself in the LORD; and He will give you the desires of your heart." This is exactly what sitting at the feet of Jesus is: delighting in Him! We gain an even richer meaning from the text when we understand the Hebrew. The word *delight* comes from the Hebrew *anag,* which is translated "pliable" or "flowing." As we relax and enjoy Jesus, in other words, our relationship with Him will be flexible and flowing—not burdensome but delightful.

Now look at the Hebrew word for *desires.* It is *ouv,* which means "union," "closeness by association" or, in its full meaning, "completeness." The psalmist discovered what Mary learned from Jesus: that if you sit at God's feet and relax in His love, you will be pliable and able to absorb new truths in order to carry them out. And when you do, you will obtain the union you desire, the closeness you crave. You will know completeness.

What a thrilling message from our Lover!

Was Jesus giving Mary license to be lazy and just sit around enjoying Him all the time? Of course not! He was showing Martha that she had missed the point of His visit. If she had discerned the importance of the moment, she might have passed over the "good" (a gourmet dinner), and prepared simpler fare, in order to obtain the "best"—the chance to sit at His feet. Jesus knew that both He and Martha needed relational intimacy that day far more than they needed a fancy meal or frantic activity.

We, too, must be careful not to miss the point of this wonderfully freeing spiritual truth. Like my driven missionary friend Fran, whose furlough schedule would have put most of us in the hospital, many women think that sitting at the feet of Jesus is unproductive time. They believe God Himself must be cracking the whip and requiring them to produce more, more, more for His Kingdom. But sitting at the feet of Jesus is productive in a different way— and much more than asking for and receiving answers. It is taking advantage of our great privilege to know Him. It is grasping hold of the majesty of His glorious nature. It is being loved and responding to that love. It is discerning His will with joyful obedience. It is worship at its loftiest plane.

Does sitting at Jesus' feet sound like an impossible task, something beyond your capabilities? Does it seem too lofty, too spiritual for mere human beings like you or me?

Jesus will never ask us to do something unless He offers help through the Holy Spirit to do it. Read on. Before this chapter ends, you will discover a section packed with practical, powerful tips for implementing our Lover's precious request. First, though, Jesus wants us to realize just how productive sitting at His feet can be.

What Are the Benefits of Sitting at His Feet?

As I have tried to make sitting at the feet of my Lover the top priority in my life, I have identified at least five fundamental benefits you and I gain from delighting in, adoring and conversing (which includes talking *and* listening) with Him.

1. Being One with Jesus

Our willingness to sit at the feet of Jesus is the first step toward the oneness with Him that He so graciously offers. Jesus wants us to be as bonded with Him as He is with the Father. Remember His declaration that "I and the Father are one" (John 10:30). The communion He modeled with His Father took priority over everything. It came before sleep, before hunger, even before circumstances. As a result Jesus' life always glorified the Father, and the works He did flowed in natural synchronization with the Father's will. Oneness. Togetherness. ". . . That they may all be one; even as Thou, Father, art in Me, and I in Thee, that they also may be in Us; that the world may believe that Thou didst send Me" (John 17:21).

Just as in marriage, oneness has the twofold aim of bringing joy to the partners and fruit (harmony of purpose, children, etc.) to the union, so oneness with Jesus brings joy to Him, joy to us and, according to this verse, the fruit of belief on the part of those who watch us.

2. Receiving More of His Love

Sitting at the feet of Jesus expands our capacity to receive His love. The more we sit at His feet, the more we learn to trust that His love motivates each of His words and actions as they touch our lives. And the more we sit at His feet, the more we absorb the truth that God Himself is love.

Trusting in His motivation of love is crucial because in the context of that love, He often points out frailties or weaknesses in our lives and characters. If our level of intimacy with Him is solid and we are secure in His acceptance, we will not be overwhelmed or distraught by His loving correction but will welcome it. We will know as cherished daughters that He is not condemning us as persons (only Satan condemns) but convicting us of behavior that does not enhance our oneness with Him.

People who really love each other feel free to be tenderly candid. Jesus longs for a relationship of trust with us that allows His candor. The closer you and I get to Him, the more He can reveal how He wants us to be like Him.

3. Sharing His Heart of Compassion

Sitting at the feet of Jesus helps us share His heart. Recall that the prophet Jonah, in his service to God, never shared God's heart. After initial resistance, he finally obeyed God and went to the wicked city of Nineveh to exhort its inhabitants to repent and turn to God. But it took being thrown overboard, being swallowed by a large fish and being vomited up on the shore for Jonah to surrender to God's direction. Even after the Ninevites listened to his message and repented, Jonah sulked outside of town. He never shared God's heart of compassion to save a people from judgment. Apparently he thought them unworthy of God's forgiveness.

Jonah obeyed God. He did his duty. But his heart was coldly unlike the warm and merciful heart of the God he served.

The older brother of the Prodigal Son, whose story is told in Luke 15, had the same cold-hearted malady. He was furious when he found out his father had offered love and forgiveness to his younger brother, who had wasted his part of the family estate and returned home penniless. The older brother had served his father faithfully but never taken time to relate to his father in love and intimacy. If he had, he might have shared the older man's heart of compassion and forgiveness and seen things from his perspective.

Jesus knows that as we sit at His feet, receiving His forgiveness, grace and acceptance, we will learn to see our world through His perspective. We will share His heart of compassion for those around us.

4. Adopting His Agenda

When we sit at the feet of Jesus, we adopt His agenda, not our own. It is important to make sure that our good deeds and service arise out of our Lover's agenda. Otherwise they become means of meeting our own needs, not the genuine needs of others.

Martha fell into this trap. Jesus' need on the day He visited her home was not for her well-intended full-course banquet. Facing Calvary, He needed her love and attention. He had things to share with her and her sister.

Martha failed to see His need because she was not sitting at His feet. Consequently she busied herself meeting her own needs for perfection and accomplishment. Then, feeling irritated and unappreciated, she ran to Jesus with her complaint about Mary. In truth she wanted *His* attention, *His* appreciation.

Sometimes we, too, want to serve Jesus—and others— on our own terms. Insensitive to His agenda, we employ as a substitute what makes us feel significant, then wonder why the whole effort turns to bitter ashes in our hands.

In our household we have often laughed about the fact that I do not have a reputation for being a good cook. I always tell people I have three main dishes that I cook reasonably well, so if they visit us for more than three days, I will have to begin repeating the menu on the fourth! You can imagine, then, that meal-planning and preparation were a real challenge for me when I had three children to care for. I did manage to keep us relatively well-nourished, but I sometimes think our children reached adulthood in spite of, not because of, my cooking.

When our children grew up, a strange thing happened. Perhaps because some of their newly acquired in-laws were renowned for their culinary expertise, I began to feel insecure about my cooking. So each time they came home to be with us during holiday times, I felt I should make a tremendous effort to prepare extra-special dishes and put on a big spread to delight and astound them.

The trouble was, while I was stuck in the kitchen trying to get a gourmet dinner together, they were bustling around the house playing games, looking at old pictures and generally enjoying each other. Meanwhile, resentment and self-pity began to build in my heart. My "good deeds" were backfiring and I felt like Martha!

My tender Lover showed me I was trying to meet a need of my own—to prove myself and compete with my children's "other parents." But my children needed me to be available to relate to them, to join in their fellowship. So I repented of my own agenda and got back onto God's. Now we are back to the three good meals I know how to make!

Even our church activities and personal ministries can stray from God's agenda and become means of meeting our own needs. I talk to many women who have neglected sitting at Jesus' feet because of their busy schedules of "doing" for Him. When they do take time to be with Him out of duty or habit, they sense no closeness, no intimacy.

We cannot fill our cups with an inch of His fullness and then expect to overflow in service for Him. A cup containing only an inch of water will never overflow!

5. Letting His Light Shine

When we sit at the feet of Jesus, His light will shine through everything we do. This benefit follows hard on the heels of number four. Jesus tells us in Matthew 5:16, "Let your light shine before men in such a way that they may see your good works, and glorify your Father who is in heaven." Does He mean people are to see only our good works? I don't think so. I believe Jesus is saying:

1. He will tell us what deeds are uniquely ours to do;
2. When we do them, people will see the light of Jesus in them.

Unsaved people do good works every day, but they are not bathed in the Spirit of our Savior. The light of Jesus within us is to shine forth in each of our good deeds, but that can happen only when our works are saturated by His Spirit as we sit at His feet. A good work alone is not enough; it is the light of Jesus *in* the good work that gives it lasting, life-changing value.

Sharon, a successful businesswoman, had received Jesus at an early age and been brought up in the Church. But she had fallen away and married while she was still out of fellowship with Jesus. Since she and her new husband both came from previously failed marriages, they decided to come back to church in the hope of stabilizing this new union.

God is faithful! Sharon experienced a wonderful renewal in Jesus, and her husband came to renewed faith one Sunday while I was preaching. What a thrill it was to watch them grow, for they did it in leaps and bounds, asking many questions and taking in the teaching eagerly at our midweek Bible study.

Everyone at Sharon's workplace began to see a remarkable difference in the way she spoke and acted. The good works to which Jesus called her at that point included lavishing love on unlovely people she met downtown. On any given Wednesday night, she would come to church with someone she had met who needed the kindness of Jesus. One man in particular stands out in my memory. Sharon took Bill under her wing, bringing him regularly to our Bible study. He was older, lame in one leg and usually wore the same disheveled clothes. Later Sharon's husband told me that, in addition to listening to Bill with interest and introducing him happily to other people in our fellowship, Sharon often laundered his shirts and prepared him homemade meals.

Yet it was not only Sharon's kindness that eventually brought Bill to saving faith in Jesus. It was the fact that Sharon was sitting at the feet of Jesus regularly, listening as He whispered to her about how much He loved Bill and wanted her to show him love, too. So Sharon's good deeds were soaked in and anointed by the Holy Spirit, and Sharon's Lover shone through each one.

Why Is Sitting at Jesus' Feet So Hard?

I have listed only a few of the benefits of sitting at Jesus' feet, but even so, wouldn't you expect Christians to be flocking to embrace such intimacy with their Lover? Instead many women (and, I am sure, men) are afraid of what personal intimacy with Jesus might mean in their lives. I have found two specific fears about intimacy with Jesus to be most common:

1. Fear of what Jesus might ask. Martha may have been afraid of being asked to do something she did not feel equipped to do. She liked to stay in the background, behind the scenes. And certainly Jesus needs people there as well as out front. But would she have been willing to move out of her comfort zone to please her Lover?

As we trust our Lover, we must be willing to become vulnerable to Him and do any new work He has for us. He may encourage you to take a step forward into unfamiliar territory because He wants your relationship with Him to grow deeper. But as His Spirit draws you closer and closer, you will find you need never fear His asking you to do something on your own. He will always equip you for the task. "Faithful is He who calls you, and He also will bring it to pass" (1 Thessalonians 5:24). If Jesus asks you to do something for His glory that threatens you momentarily, keep listening and trusting. He has gone before you, He has been there and He will be with you as you obey.

2. *Fear of not getting all our tasks done.* Another common fear about sitting at the feet of Jesus is that too much time spent there will prevent us from doing all that we know we must do. It is hard to accept the truth that no service we can render our Lover is greater than that of building our relationship with Him.

"But Jan," you say, "don't you remember all those commands in the Word—to go, to tell, to do?"

Of course I remember. But all of what we do must grow out of our relational intimacy with Jesus. Remember, our service must be the overflow of what we hear and learn in our close union with Him, or it will not glorify Him and it will not last.

Two familiar verses speak to this issue:

> For by grace you have been saved through faith; and that not of yourselves, it is the gift of God; not as a result of works, that no one should boast.
>
> Ephesians 2:8–9

How marvelous to know that we can do nothing to merit our salvation! It is God's free gift to each of us who trusts Christ.

Then verse 10 gives light as to what God expects once we receive His precious gift of forgiveness and eternal life:

> For we are His workmanship, created in Christ Jesus for good works, which God prepared beforehand, that we should walk in them.

The new life in us is the creative workmanship of God Himself. He does not patch up our old life; He gives us a new one (see 2 Corinthians 5:17), and picked out certain works for us to do long before we came to know Him as Savior. These are especially designed for us by Him, but we will not know what they are if we fail to sit at His feet. We cannot divorce sitting at His feet from discovering these works, and we will discover them only in our relationship with Him—in the listening and absorbing, in the quiet voice of His Spirit. At His feet we learn in wonder who we really are and what He has planned for us to do that will bring Him glory.

While Martha hustled about preparing something for her guest to eat, Mary was loving Him and listening to His voice. We do not know all that Jesus shared with her that day, but we know that later on she was able to do something for Him that blessed Him and brought honor to her. Perhaps it was in the intimacy of those moments at His feet that Jesus told her about His impending death. Perhaps He shared with this woman of Bethany the deep distress in His spirit concerning all that was yet to take place. The apostles missed out on this intimate sharing in the Garden of Gethsemane because they could not stay awake to watch with Jesus and participate in His ordeal.

Mary, on the other hand, somehow shared His burden because she sat at His feet. We know this because it was she who came to Jesus before He went to the cross, and poured costly perfume and pure nard over His head (see John 12:1–8; Mark 14:3–9). Some there thought she had wasted this expensive ointment, but Jesus rose to her defense. He announced to the crowd not only that she had done a good thing, but that "she has anointed My body beforehand for the burial" (Mark 14:8).

Perhaps Mary's kind deed sprang from what she learned while sitting at Jesus' feet. It was probably one of the good works ordained for Mary by the Lord Himself! Out of their deep communion, Mary discerned a need, and in her love for Jesus, she met it.

This is what sitting at His feet should do for all of us. Our good works will come as a result of our intimacy, and they will be just the ones He wants us to do.

Jesus Paid the Price for Our Intimacy

Few worthwhile pursuits come without cost. Just as we enjoy deep friendship with another human being at the cost of giving our time and ourselves, so it costs us to enjoy intimacy with Jesus—in time, in determination and in giving up the good in order to get the best. We must decide if we are willing to pay the price.

It is helpful to recall what it cost Jesus to bring us the opportunity for intimacy. Before He died on the cross, human beings did not have access to God in the same way we do now. In Old Testament times, only the high priest could go into the Holy of Holies, that place in the Temple where God's presence resided and where the treasured Ark of the Covenant and mercy seat were. Once a year the high priest entered the area, separated by a veil from top to bottom, in order to make atonement for his own sins and for the sins of the people.

Coming into the presence of the living God was such an awesome experience that each priest had a rope with a bell tied around him so people outside could hear him moving around. If God did not accept the sacrifice and the priest died, he could be pulled from the chamber by the rope, so that no one else had to risk the displeasure of God by entering the Holy of Holies. Approaching God personally was out of the question.

This system remained in effect until Jesus came and fulfilled all the requirements of God's demand for holiness. When Jesus shed His blood on the cross for our sins and the sins of the world, and when He breathed His last breath, our relationship with almighty God changed forever. The Bible says that at that very moment, "the veil of the temple was torn in two from top to bottom" (Mark 15:38). In this dramatic way God demonstrated His pleasure in removing the sin that stood between us and Him, and told us that from now on we could come boldly, confidently and with the assurance of His love and acceptance into His presence.

Sitting at the feet of Jesus is not a casual experience. But we can come confidently, reverently and filled with awe to build the intimacy our Lover died to give us. On the basis of the redemption He won for us at Calvary, we can "come boldly unto the throne of grace, that we may obtain mercy, and find grace to help in time of need" (Hebrews 4:16, KJV).

How costly it is for us to neglect sitting at the feet of Jesus! We cannot afford to lose touch with His tenderness, His personal presence in our lives. The price we pay to be with Him could never measure up to the price Jesus paid to give us this new and wonderful liberty.

How to Sit at Jesus' Feet

One of the last things I talked about with my friend Fran when we had lunch together during her furlough was how to cultivate the practice of sitting at the feet of Jesus.

"How can we change old habits and patterns?" Fran asked. "How do we know for sure the things Jesus has planned for us to do?"

Since Fran's questions are probably yours, too, let's look at three practical tips that can make sitting at the feet of Jesus a reality in your life and mine.

1. Ask Yourself Four Questions

Here are four questions we should ask ourselves:

1. Does Jesus consider my relationship with Him warm, loving and intimate?
2. What would He change about our relationship?
3. Is my intimacy with Jesus evident to others?
4. Are the things I do for Him coming from what I hear in our closeness?

It is important to take some time to ask Jesus these questions, too. Write down anything you sense from Him as you read His Word and listen to His Holy Spirit.

2. Learn to Tarry in His Presence

Tarry is an old word, not used much anymore. It means to wait or linger. We must linger in order to hear Jesus and open our hearts to behold Him. But we cannot always do this because of the clamor of our busy lives. We are easily distracted, and the very nature of what we are doing for His Kingdom may have brought us to a place of exhaustion and burnout.

Jesus sees our hearts and realizes our honest passion, but He calls us back continually to the quietness of His voice.

The prophet Elijah is a wonderful example of someone who almost forgot to tarry. First Kings 18 tells the story of one of the great spiritual moments in Elijah's life, when he called for a showdown between the false prophets of Baal, worshiped by King Ahab and his wife, Jezebel, and the God of Abraham, Isaac and Jacob.

Elijah allowed the false prophets of Baal, gathering on Mount Carmel, to set up a sacrifice and call on their god to consume it with fire. All morning they did so, yelling and cutting themselves in their attempt to get Baal's attention—to no avail. Elijah taunted and teased them, suggesting their god might be asleep or otherwise occupied.

Then Elijah took his turn. He built an altar, covered it with wood and dug a trench around the altar deep enough to hold about eight gallons of water. He cut up an ox for the sacrifice and poured copious amounts of water over the altar, the wood and the sacrifice—so much so that the trench was filled, too. Then this faithful servant called on the one true God of Israel, who sent down fire from heaven. It licked up all the water and consumed the sacrifice in a thrilling victory for the one true God.

The people watching shouted in amazement that the Lord was indeed God. All the prophets of Baal were killed, and Elijah took one more step of trust: He declared that a rainstorm would soon come to soak the nation, which had been plagued with drought for three and a half years.

God answered once again, the rains came and Elijah hurried off to the valley of Jezreel, knowing that King Ahab and his queen would be furious with him. Sure enough, Jezebel sent a messenger to tell Elijah she was going to kill him. And at this point Elijah collapsed in body, mind and spirit.

Think about what he had been through. He had put his life on the line by calling for a showdown with the prophets of Baal. Had the outcome been different, Elijah would actually have died on Mount Carmel. Nor could he have known the outcome ahead of time, since he had no Old Testament in which to read the story. But he trusted God in a stress-filled, tense situation that the Bible says lasted for hours. His body and emotions probably felt as if they had gone through a wringer. By the time it was all over, he must have felt spent.

(No matter how strong our passion is for Jesus, or how zealous our works, we, too, are prime candidates for depression and anxiety when we are worn out physically and emotionally. The devil waits patiently for us to come to this point and then pounces, knowing how vulnerable we are.)

What happened next is one of the most tender accounts of God's love and concern to be found anywhere in Scripture. An angel touched Elijah and said, "Arise, eat" (1 Kings 19:5). He looked up and found a bread cake still warm from baking and a jug of water. He ate and drank. Then the angel came again, telling him to eat more since he was to go on a journey. Elijah obeyed and blurted out to God all his fears, disappointments, self-pity and exhaustion.

At this juncture God could have done several things. He could have left Elijah alone until he was feeling better about life. He could have snapped His fingers and told Elijah that people who belong to Him are not allowed to feel discouraged (not to mention suicidal), so he should shape up and get moving. But He did neither of these.

No one understands our humanity as God does! God had ministered to Elijah's physical body, and now He was going to minister to his spirit.

"Go . . . stand on the mountain before the LORD," God told Elijah (verse 11). Elijah obeyed. First God sent a wind so strong that it broke up pieces of the mountain. "But the LORD was not in the wind" (verse 11). Next God allowed an earthquake to rattle the ground, but He was not in the earthquake either. Finally God sent "a sound of a gentle blowing" (verse 12), and in this stillness Elijah heard the voice of God. He was reached by the quietness of the Spirit.

How glorious and precious is God's quietness! There is no substitute for it and no shortcut to it. We must get away from the work, the duties and whatever vies for our attention so that the gentle breeze of His Spirit can renew, refresh and instruct us as we sit at Jesus' feet. We must tarry so that despair can be replaced with hope.

3. Develop Your Own Ways to Enjoy His Presence

There are many ways to enter the Lord's presence. I have no wish to develop a formula, as different approaches work for different people with different personalities.

I like to take a chair and put it directly across from where I am sitting. I sense Jesus in the other chair and gaze upon Him in my heart. I talk to Him, and then I listen.

What would you like to say to Jesus if He were in a chair across from you right now? One woman told me, "I don't want to say anything. I just want Him to hold me close because I'm so tired and worn out!"

If that is your need, let Him hold you. Look at Him. What does He see in your heart and in your eyes? Share it with Him and listen to His encouraging words.

For some women, the outdoors is a good place to sit at the feet of Jesus. They love the fresh air, the breezes and the sight of His creation. If this sounds like you, maybe you would like to take a walk with Him, holding your Lover's hand, laughing and enjoying His company.

One young mother told me it was difficult to find a place to be with Jesus where her children could not follow her. "The bathroom is my only place of solace," she laughed, "but Jesus and I have some wonderful times together there!"

Perhaps it will help you to keep a special notebook to record what you believe Jesus is saying to you during these times at His feet. Tarry. Let Him speak to you through His Word and Spirit. Let Him help you release those things that are less important, and decide on the works He has planned for you.

Jesus is a faithful Lover. He will help you persevere in your times at His feet. He will cause you to come with great anticipation to these times in His presence. If you are willing, He will help you hunger and thirst for more and more of Him. Tarry until you know the time has come for you to get up and be about His business.

Will You Choose the Better Part?

Jesus said something to Martha, while her sister was sitting at His feet, that is worth repeating. He said, "Mary has chosen the good part, which shall not be taken away from her" (Luke 10:42).

We must never forget that the relationship we build with our Lover now goes on into eternity with us. Sitting at His feet has eternal value.

We must by necessity do much that will ultimately pass away, but we must always weigh the eternal with the temporal. I doubt that when I am about to die, I will regret not doing one more chore or attending one more meeting. But I do not want to regret spending too little time at the feet of Jesus.

Our new life in the Spirit with our Lover, Jesus, should be a progressive romantic adventure. Sitting at the feet of Jesus will make it so. Whatever He tells us to do as we listen, we can do with confidence and joy, sensing His pleasure. Why? Because being with Him will give us the right focus and priorities.

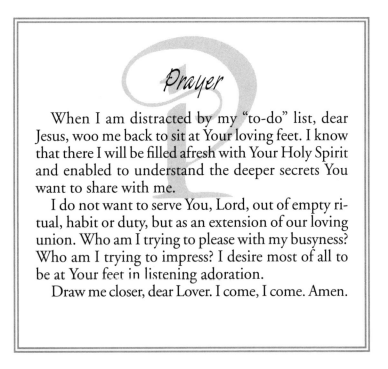

Prayer

When I am distracted by my "to-do" list, dear Jesus, woo me back to sit at Your loving feet. I know that there I will be filled afresh with Your Holy Spirit and enabled to understand the deeper secrets You want to share with me.

I do not want to serve You, Lord, out of empty ritual, habit or duty, but as an extension of our loving union. Who am I trying to please with my busyness? Who am I trying to impress? I desire most of all to be at Your feet in listening adoration.

Draw me closer, dear Lover. I come, I come. Amen.

9

He Weeps with You

One of my hopes for every human being is enjoying the blessing of a truly good friend. I mean the kind who knows all your warts but loves you just the same; the kind who listens when you need to talk and sits in silence when there are no words; the kind who rejoices when you rejoice and weeps when you weep (see Romans 12:15).

Nancy was that kind of friend. She and I had lots of things in common, right down to the fact that we each had three children who were almost identical in ages. We spent many hours together at Little League games when our boys were young, and our families ate pancakes together at our favorite restaurant after church each Sunday. As we were renewed in the Lord, our friendship grew deeper as we began to pray together and share the ups and downs of raising our youngsters.

It was Nancy who sat with me at the hospital hour after hour when our son, Andrew, went through the most fearful and trying ordeal of his young life—major cancer surgery. One day Nancy led me outside Andy's room at the hospital.

"Jan," she said, her face wet with tears, "I could never stand to watch my child suffer like this!"

I told her God had given me exactly the grace I needed, almost like a spiritual anesthetic.

God healed Andrew miraculously and Nancy celebrated with us. But I will never forget the comfort she offered by weeping with me through that difficult time.

Years ago you may have earned a gold star in Sunday school for memorizing the shortest verse in the Bible: "Jesus wept" (John 11:35). The Scriptures make only one other mention of Jesus' weeping—in Luke 19:41, where we are told that He wept over Jerusalem and her rejection of Him. It was a rejection symbolic of the one exercised by so many of God's chosen people, the Israelites, in the past and on into the present, and it gave Jesus deep pain.

It astounds me and fills me with awe to think of the great Creator of the universe weeping, feeling anguish, sorrowing as His creatures sorrow. The tender display of Jesus' incarnation is underlined when we understand and accept an amazing fact: Our Lover, Jesus, weeps for us and with us as we experience the heartaches and sorrows of life.

In the last chapter I pointed to specific fears we may have about intimacy with our Lover. He sees our faint-heartedness. He realizes our fears of rejection, our insecurities, our feelings of unworthiness. And He knows the wounds inflicted on us by people who have failed us.

But if we shrink from the intimacy He offers, we may miss the comfort of His weeping. Our Lover is patient as we learn to trust Him and the various dimensions of our relationship with Him more deeply. Not only does He go before us in triumph and joy. Not only does He give us new names, genuine self-esteem, freedom from bondage and focused priorities to ease the pain of our aching place. He also weeps with us as we brave the journey.

Sorrow Comes to Bethany

We have already noted the special relationship Jesus had with Mary, Martha and Lazarus of Bethany. Just as His interactions with the sisters show us the importance of letting Him help us choose to sit at His feet, so another incident in His friendship with them demonstrates how our Lover weeps when we weep.

The incident began when Lazarus, the brother of Mary and Martha, fell ill at home. Almost immediately, it seems, the sisters sent a message to Jesus: "Lord . . . he whom You love is sick" (John 11:3). Their relationship was so close, so familiar, that they apparently felt no need to say, "Please come." They just assumed He would.

But when Jesus heard the news, He did not drop everything and rush to Lazarus' side. The Bible tells us this in a curious way. First we read that Jesus received the message (see verse 4); then we read that He loved Mary, Martha and Lazarus (see verse 5); and then:

> When therefore He heard that he was sick, He stayed then two days longer in the place where He was.
>
> verse 6

It seems a strange reaction to such urgent and heartbreaking news from friends in His inner circle! Can you imagine what Mary and Martha went through as they waited by Lazarus' bedside? When they first sent word to the Lord about their brother's illness, he was alive; they had hope. How endless each day must have seemed as they waited for the Master to come! "Why isn't He here yet?" they must have said to each other. "Why does He delay?"

Finally, from a human and medical standpoint, it was too late. Lazarus was dead.

That is when Jesus finally got to Bethany. He encountered Martha first—spent with waiting, overcome with grief, angry with Him.

She blurted out, "Lord, if You had been here, my brother would not have died" (verse 21). She tried to summon up words of faith—"Even now I know that whatever You ask of God, God will give you" (verse 22)—but the words came out automatically, dutifully, even patronizingly.

Jesus offered no excuses for His delay. Instead He spent the next several minutes trying to focus Martha back to faith, before she went off to find Mary with the news of His arrival.

When Mary met Jesus, she fell at His feet and repeated Martha's plaintive cry: "Lord, if You had been here, my brother would not have died" (verse 32).

It would have been only human for the sisters to feed one another's doubt, hopelessness and, yes, anger at the Friend they thought would never let them down.

The Bible says that Mary's weeping, and the empathetic weeping of her friends and neighbors, moved Jesus deeply and troubled Him.

"Where have you laid him?" Jesus asked (verse 34). "Come and see" was the reply. At this point Jesus broke down, entering fully into the heartache and tragedy.

Why did Jesus cry? Why was He moved and troubled when He saw Lazarus' family and friends in the throes of a grief He knew would be short-lived? After all, Jesus knew His Father would raise Lazarus from the dead. He knew it even before He and His disciples had left the place He was visiting to answer Mary and Martha's summons.

As our sovereign God, Jesus sees "the end from the beginning" (Isaiah 46:10). He knows that His plans for each of us will ultimately be a source of rejoicing, regardless of Satan's attempts to dismay, distract and harm us. But the marvelous message of this chapter is that even though Jesus sees the healing, grace and help that lie ahead on each of our paths, His mercy is still abundantly available to help us through our suffering. His sovereign knowledge will never negate His compassion. He will not let us go through our woundedness alone even though He knows the final, triumphant outcome for each hurtful situation in our lives.

As our Lover, Jesus feels what we feel because He loves us and aches to see us in pain. Jesus wept for the sorrow and, I believe, for the short-sighted, failed faith of Mary and Martha. He weeps for your sorrow and human frailty, and for mine.

This tender aspect of our Lover's nature, His ability to reach our aching places with His love-initiated salvation, drew us to Him in the first place. In the context of our intimate relationship with Him, He weeps with each of us in any area of our lives in which we feel pain.

When We Walk through the Storm

What can we learn from Mary and Martha to help us appropriate the comfort our Lover offers when our aching places overflow with grief? How can we learn to walk creatively, constructively through life's storms arm in arm with the Lover who understands—and will never dismiss as insignificant—our tears?

I see three principles in the story of Lazarus' death for handling life's heartaches. What pleasure we will give our Lover as we learn to apply them in our lives!

1. Believe in Your Heart That God Is in Control

How easy it is to forget this most basic of principles! Like Martha, we often need to be brought back to the reality of His power, sovereignty and love. Jesus' response to Martha's disappointment over His delay has become the victory cry for believers down through the ages:

> "I am the resurrection and the life; he who believes in Me shall live even if he dies, and everyone who lives and believes in Me shall never die."
>
> John 11:25–26

Faced with Martha's honest frustration, grief and failed expectations, Jesus did not take time to go into the many reasons she should have chosen to trust Him. Instead He cut to the chase with this magnificent truth about who He is and what Martha could expect from Him.

The bottom line of our faith in Him and our relationship with Him is His ability to bring us back from death to spiritual, experiential and eternal life. If He can do that—and as God of the universe He most certainly can!—is anything else too difficult for Him? Of course not. He is in control.

Do not make the mistake of mouthing the words out of rote duty or pat piety. Instead, let your thoughts, words and actions show your Lover and the world that you are proceeding on the premise that He is in control.

2. Learn to Wait on—and for—Jesus

As I look back on my freshman year at a Christian college, I realize what an impetuous young damsel I was! That year the girls in my dorm had a grievance against the school that we took up with the dean of women: We were not going to put up with rough toilet paper any longer. We wanted to be heard, and we wanted action!

We were promised that those in charge of operations would be notified of our concern. After waiting for a few days but hearing nothing, we took the matter into our own hands. Enlisting the help of willing cohorts on a Saturday night, we gathered as many rolls of the hated tissue as we could find, diverted our dormmates and sneaked into their rooms to unroll the toilet paper out their windows.

The night was windy, and by early Sunday morning most of the toilet paper had scattered to cover the chapel, lawn, trees, bushes and everything else on campus. At 6:05 A.M. the college president, who had arisen early to take a walk before morning worship, came to the dorm. He was not pleased, and every girl in the dorm was enrolled promptly to clean up the mess.

No one ever told who had instigated the mini-rebellion. But to this day Jesus, with His great sense of humor, uses my failure to wait expectantly for new toilet paper to remind me not to run ahead of Him or become weary with His delay.

All of us feel frustrated when we think Jesus is not responding to our needs the way we think He should. Waiting is always hard, and the longer the delay, the more vulnerable we are to hopelessness and despair. We wonder if the Lord has heard us, or if He understands how urgently we need His help. We may even begin to suspect that He does not intend to answer because He is upset with us. Perhaps He is delaying purposefully because of an offense we cannot even remember.

Satan plants all kinds of erroneous thoughts like these as we go through hard times. We need to guard against his deceitful insinuations by knowing God's Word and understanding how God works so we do not hurt Him by falling into the depression and faithlessness that came on Mary and Martha.

From a human perspective, even short periods of time seem to drag when we are waiting. You are familiar with this phenomenon if you have ever waited the five to seven minutes it usually takes for an ambulance to arrive at the scene of an emergency. Concurrently we can be tempted to feel that we can accomplish nothing while we wait; that idleness and listlessness are our only options.

But waiting on and for Jesus does not imply idle sitting. It actually means *active endurance.* While we wait, our Lover wants us to do two important things:

First, *He wants us to look at His past record of faithfulness and expect that He will be true to His own nature and character.* "Remember all the way which the LORD your God has led you," God told the Israelites over and over (Deuteronomy 8:2; see also 15:15; 16:3; 32:6–9; 1 Chronicles 16:12). Despite the rich heritage of miraculous intervention that God wove into Israel's life as a nation and as individuals, His people failed to give Him credit for being a faithful Lover who always came through for them. Instead they treated Him with suspicion at each new turn in the road.

I don't know about you, but I would be hurt and insulted if my husband overlooked my record of forty years of faithful marriage and assumed I was having an affair every time I was late getting home! Yet that is how we often treat our Lover, overlooking His history of constancy and almost expecting Him to let us down. As we wait on and for Jesus, we need to do so expectantly, knowing He will always come through for us in the very best way.

The second thing our Lover wants us to do while we wait is *trust actively that He is behind the scenes working out every element of every situation for our growth and long-term benefit.* Romans 8:28 could not be any clearer:

> We know that God causes all things to work together for good to those who love God, to those who are called according to His purpose.

Remember, we belong to the God who took a young man named Joseph from near-death and slavery to the second-highest position in Egypt (see Genesis 37–45). We have been bought by the Lord who took an embarrassing shortage of wine at a wedding in Cana of Galilee and turned it into a triumph of hospitality (see John 2).

When we wait for our Lover with active endurance, we bring Him pride and joy.

3. Learn to Trust His Timing

"God's timing is perfect." How often have we heard that statement but relegated it to our store of theological clichés?

Do we actually believe it? We need to bank on it in times of delay.

What was Jesus doing during the time He stayed away from Bethany—that agonizing time during which Mary and Martha watched their brother slip away from them? He was interceding for Lazarus and discerning the Father's will.

How do we know this? First of all, we know the pattern Jesus followed in other situations. He always sought His Father's will, for He came to do only His Father's will and not His own (see John 4:34). Habitually He spent time in prayer before making a decision. Second, we know Jesus was interceding for Lazarus because of His own words when He arrived at Lazarus' tomb: "Father, I thank Thee that Thou heardest Me" (John 11:41). He then yelled for Lazarus to come out of the grave. He was not asking His Father at that time to do the miracle. He had already settled the matter in intercession before He arrived. All He needed to do now was thank God for His miraculous answer, and He did so out loud in order to activate the faith of those who were listening.

When Jesus delays in answering your cry for help, He is not doing so to frustrate you. He is interceding for you. The answer will come in His perfect way and time, because God *is* always on time. This truth (which we will explore in the next chapter) is well put by Solomon: "He has made everything appropriate [or beautiful] in its time" (Ecclesiastes 3:11).

Jesus Weeps When . . .

Because our humanity can grasp concepts better when they are illustrated by examples with which we can identify, let's look at four specific life circumstances in which Jesus weeps with you and me.

1. Jesus Weeps When You Mourn

Despite the fact that our Lover sees death as a doorway—a passage into eternity in which our eyes and ears will see and hear infinite glory—His empathetic caring is always evident when we lose a loved one. He knows that while the one who has died is now in the hands of a loving and just God, we are left with aching hearts to endure unimaginable hurt and loneliness. So it was that when Isaiah announced the coming of the Messiah, he said God anointed Him "to comfort all who mourn" (Isaiah 61:2).

I have heard women describe the loss of a mate as similar to the loss of an arm or leg. Especially when a woman and her husband knew oneness in the Lord, but even when they did not, his death leaves her feeling fragmented, broken, like a shadow of her former self.

If you have lost a spouse through death or divorce, Jesus knows and understands. He will weep with you as you go through this valley of loss. He will sit with you until the sorrow is bearable, until the ache lessens. If your mate is now with Him, He will offer the promise that someday you will see not only your heavenly Lover face to face, but your earthly one as well. If your husband has abandoned you, He will grieve with you the loss of your dreams, your home, your anticipated future of togetherness. In both cases He promises, "I know the plans that I have for you, plans . . . to give you a future and a hope" (Jeremiah 29:11).

Even more, Jesus stands ready to become your Husband as you heal from the loss of your mate. You can feel secure in His protective arms. With the help of your compassionate Lover, you do not have to hurry the healing process but can allow each stage of grief to bring further grace. You can stay in the arms of Jesus for solace and renewed strength, then rise up to adjust, to return to living with hope and purpose.

Perhaps you have lost a child—a loss hard to fathom, because to outlive our children these days seems unnatural; it goes against the grain. Again, Jesus weeps with you in your anguish. No one understands the loss of a child more than God does. He gave His only Son willingly, knowing He would die an excruciating death for the sins of the world. Heaven was torn asunder the day God's Son shed His blood at Calvary, and the Father's heart was broken for His Child. So He understands this loss in a personal way.

One morning some years ago I was at home in bed, hooked up to a traction apparatus to relieve the pressure on my ailing back. When the phone on my night table rang, I picked it up to hear a strained, muffled voice at the other end say, "This is Nancy."

My good friend's voice was hardly recognizable as she told me that her son, Richard, had been killed in an automobile accident on his way back to college, the innocent victim of a drunk driver.

I remember dizziness and a strange kind of whirring all around me. Flinging off the traction apparatus, I flew into action, stopping first for a prayer from our daughter, Shannon, that quieted my spirit and lifted my immobility.

Dave and I and our children did all we could to help Nancy, her husband, Chuck, and Richard's siblings through the next few days. I remember in particular the moment Chuck saw Dave at the funeral home. Suddenly Chuck was able to release the pain and tension of trying to be strong for his family. He ran into Dave's embrace, and I heard a lament from the depths of his soul, the cry of a stricken father wailing into my husband's chest. Dave rocked Chuck gently as they stood there, and I knew Jesus was in the midst of that huddle, sharing Chuck's grief in his terrible loss.

After a beautiful, touching funeral, and following a family gathering at Chuck and Nancy's home, Nancy made a startling request.

"Jan," she asked calmly, "will you go into Richard's room and get his guitar?"

I had taught Richard to play that guitar, and could not believe she wanted me to play it now. But she did. Nancy wanted us to sing songs of praise and enter an attitude of worship. So I began to play.

As we lifted our voices quietly to the Lord, singing and crying intermittently, something remarkable happened. Jesus was in our midst, the Holy One of God. He wrapped Himself around each of us in that moment, and I could feel His tears washing over me with mercy and power. He was weeping with us at the close of a wonderful and heart-breaking day, and He continued to weep with us in the months to come.

Our Lover is a most merciful Savior. We cannot always understand why things happen as they do. We live in a fallen world in which believers are not immune to the disease, reckless behavior and poor judgment that result from sin. We are not spared heartache and loss. But we have One who goes through each step with us, aware of our suffering, conscious of every tear.

2. Jesus Weeps with You When You Fall

We are human, easily led astray, prone to step out of fellowship with others and with our Lover. And all too often, because we have a warped perception of God, we allow our sin to estrange us from the very One who longs to soothe our aching places and restore us to our familiar place at His feet.

Author J. B. Phillips' book *Your God Is Too Small* deals with various false, unbiblical conceptions of God. Note how sensibly he treats the unbiblical standard of morbid perfectionism we all too often feel God expects of us—a standard we allow to keep us out of fellowship with our Lover:

Of all the false gods there is probably no greater nuisance in the spiritual world than the "god of one hundred per cent." For He is plausible. It can so easily be argued that since God is Perfection, and since He asks the complete loyalty of His creatures, then the best way of serving, pleasing and worshipping Him is to set up absolute one-hundred-per-cent standards and see to it that we obey them. After all, did not Christ say, "Be ye perfect"?

Phillips goes on to point out that Christianity is not a performance but a way of life:

To "learn" implies growth . . . the making and correcting of mistakes . . . a steady upward progress toward an ideal. The "perfection" to which Christ commands men to progress is this ideal. The modern high-pressure Christian of certain circles would like to impose perfection of one hundred per cent as a set of rules to be immediately enforced, instead of as a shining ideal to be faithfully pursued. . . . Such a distortion of Christian truth could not possibly originate from the One who said His "yoke was easy" and His "burden light." . . . To imagine that He will have no dealings with [Christians] until they are prepared to give Him perfect devotion is just another manifestation of the "god of one hundred per cent." . . . Who would deny the father's interest in the prodigal son when his Spiritual Index was at a very low figure indeed?

Some women cannot believe Jesus can restore them fully once they have fallen. This suggests, of course, that they were in a state of perfection to begin with, while our only claim to perfection is through the covering of Jesus' own righteousness with which He clothes us at salvation.

Satan would like us to believe, on the other hand, that when we fall, we will be Jesus' stepdaughters when we return to His arms, never wholly accepted as we once were. In this state of mind we lose motivation to return to Him because we are out of fellowship, confused and easy prey to the deception of the enemy.

If you have fallen away, Jesus weeps for you and with you. He did not come to this earth to condemn you but to save you (see John 3:17). He mourns when you are unwilling to give up your sin and receive forgiveness and restoration. He weeps when you fall away from intimacy with Him through temptation or disobedience, feeling lost in confusion and deception. Your Lover is right where you are, ready at this moment to forgive whatever you have done and restore you fully to His arms of love and security. He will never save partially; He can only save wholly and completely.

I am always touched by the story of the woman caught in adultery. Envision yourself in her skin on that degrading day. You are seized from the bed of the man you have slept with (not your husband) and dragged half-naked into the streets, where people condemn you for your sin. You know they may decide to stone you to death. Shamed, alone, guilty, terrified, you try to hide your exposed body, but it is useless. You cover your face with your hands and crouch down in the dirt.

Then Jesus of Nazareth comes on the scene. The crowd is hushed at first by His presence, then tries to get Him to agree that you ought to be stoned. But Jesus reminds them of their own sin and hypocrisy before God. The crowd begins to disperse. Then He turns His attention to you.

To your amazement, He takes off His cloak, lifts you up and wraps it gently around you. He is tender and kind. You do not deserve such kindness! But looking into His eyes, you find not condemnation but forgiveness and love.

"Where are they?" He asks. "Did no one condemn you?"

"No one, Lord," you reply.

"Neither do I condemn you; go your way; from now on sin no more" (John 8:10–11).

He has given you a brand-new start!

How about *you*? Have you succumbed to temptation? Do you feel ashamed and guilty? Jesus weeps for you and wants to restore you, to lift you up and cover you with His cloak—His blood shed on your behalf. You can dare come home to Him. You are forever His cherished daughter.

3. Jesus Weeps for Your Unbelief

Just before Jesus gave the shout that raised Lazarus from the dead, Martha reminded Him that her brother had been dead four days, that his decaying body would stink. Her statement astounds me, and it must have frustrated Jesus. He had just spent time focusing her back to faith. He had proclaimed Himself the One able to cause all who believe in Him to live forever. She had seen this Man she loved do other extraordinary miracles. Why was she unable to believe Him fully at this graveside testing?

True to His nature, Jesus did not embarrass or condemn Martha. Gently He reminded her of their earlier conversation, then simply went ahead and raised her brother from the dead.

Our Lover is gentle with our unbelief as well, and weeps for us when we cannot bring ourselves to trust His promises totally. He knows that our aching places are in the process of healing and that it takes time to learn to take Him at His Word.

But every day we have new opportunities to trust Jesus or to doubt; to depend on Him or to take things into our own hands. If we begin trusting Him with the smaller items that plague our daily living, we can graduate to trusting Him for the larger ones.

What in your life seems impossible for Jesus to do? Tell Him how you feel. Admit your doubt. He knows all about it anyway, but longs to have you sit at His feet and share it with Him. Let Him tell you what His Word says about it, and then ask Him to send you someone who has experienced this need and can help you through it. Remember, 2 Corinthians 1:4 reminds us that God

> comforts us in all our affliction so that we may be able to comfort those who are in any affliction with the comfort with which we ourselves are comforted by God.

This principle plays itself out in our lives over and over. Once you have been lifted up and strengthened, Jesus will use you later to help someone else.

Like Martha, we, too, have seen Jesus perform many wonderful deeds. But in a crisis we fear and fail to believe that He will come through for us. Our Lover understands. He looked at Martha that day at the tomb and demonstrated before her His authority and power. He had already wept for her unbelief, and now He moved to meet her need.

Don't let your unbelief dominate you. Struggle with it honestly. Our Lover will not turn away when faith fails you temporarily, but will, if you let Him, focus you back to faith. He has all the power to raise you from the death of failed faith, hopelessness and despair. The more you trust, the fuller your fellowship with Him will be as you sit at His feet.

4. Jesus Weeps with Us Over the World's Brokenness

Jesus weeps with us over the havoc that the selfishness and sin of others have worked in our lives, and in the lives of all the people in the world. He yearns for us to be brokenhearted over the same things that break His heart. He weeps

- for wounded marriages and for the selfishness and pride that keep husbands and wives from forgiving each other;
- for the children and adults who suffer or die each year from emotional, physical and sexual abuse;

- for the babies slaughtered each year by abortion;
- for Western nations abundantly blessed yet dissociating themselves at alarming rates from His moral standards;
- for nations in the developing world lost in poverty, hunger and spiritual darkness;
- for people who push Jesus into the background and refuse to make Him Lord of their lives;
- for those who deny Him in the workplace, refusing to take a stand for holiness;
- for His Church and those within it who keep Him standing on the outside;
- for those who rush to cults and other false religions because they have not been reached, or have been hurt, by the Church.

Susan's Story

Susan's heartbreaking story represents the pain and lostness from which Jesus longs to free millions in the world who do not know Him. I write about her because you may recognize some of your own pain as you view her life, and you may sense our Lover's tender desire to touch you as He touched her. Or perhaps you will see in Susan's pain a mirror of someone else's, and hear our Lover's call for you to be a conduit of His healing.

I prayed with Susan at a conference one afternoon, beginning a relationship that has spanned several years.

Her first concern was a lack of assurance that she was born again. I talked with her about what receiving Jesus' love and salvation into her life meant. She thought she had asked Him into her heart, but had no confidence that He had accepted her. As we talked further, I realized Susan needed more than just an afternoon of prayer.

We did not live in the same city, so in the weeks and months that followed, we talked through letters and phone calls, meeting occasionally for lunch. As her story unfolded, I was sickened and grieved.

Susan had grown up in a home that professed Christianity. Her grandfather was a minister and her mother was active in their local church. From all appearances, Susan's environment was stable. But when she was two years old, she fell through an unfastened screen out of a second-story window.

She could not remember how long she had to stay in the hospital or how long her at-home recovery lasted. But she tensed up when she told me about the incident, believing it had triggered an onslaught of circumstances that ruled her life from then on.

Why? Because Susan's mother, feeling guilty over the fall, began to exercise an unhealthy control over her daughter's life. Susan was not encouraged to play with other children for fear she might get hurt. She never learned to relate socially to other youngsters, was teased about her looks and shyness and got into fights. Understandably Susan began to retreat into a world of her own, convinced by her mother that she was different.

Susan's mother, unskilled in helping her daughter grow in self-confidence, often made the mistake of comparing her with other children at church. "Why can't you be like them?" she would nag. And, "What will people think of our family if you make poor grades at school?"

"I never let anyone into my world," Susan confided to me, "not even Jesus." She had heard about Him since she was little, had gone to church and even accepted Him as Savior when she went to church camp as a young teenager.

"At first I was excited and felt good about what I had done," she told me. "But no one taught me how to have a personal relationship with Him." She sighed. "Once I got back home, the good feeling was gone and nothing had changed. I thought Jesus had rejected me, like everyone else."

As I came to know Susan, I noticed her haunting disconnectedness from some emotions, and her inability to cry, contrasted with occasional uncontrollable outbursts of anger. Sometimes I received letters in which she unleashed vitriolic language against me—language I had never heard before. She was convinced I would eventually abandon her.

I knew Susan needed the help of a licensed therapist, but was not sure she would seek or receive such help. I also knew she needed to transfer her dependency to Jesus, and perceived that He had placed me in her life to care about her and lead her to His love and healing. I ignored each angry letter, and soon Susan would send an apology. "I don't know why I do that, Jan," she would lament. "I don't mean those things, but they just pour out."

Finally Susan began to reveal the source of her confusion and pain. By the time she had reached her late teens, she had made few friends and had never worked. Her mother told her it would be hard for her to hold down a job because of her shy, withdrawn personality. Her parents did allow her to date a young man they knew, but on one unforgettable night he date-raped her. Susan was afraid to tell her parents for fear they would blame her, but finally risked confiding the experience because she thought she was pregnant.

Her mother wrung her hands in despair, calling the whole situation a disgrace to the family. Her father, shaking his head in disgust, told her she was "spoiled goods" and would never marry. Both parents did blame her for the incident and made her promise to tell no one.

It turned out she was not pregnant, and the young man was never confronted. Filled with bewilderment, Susan retreated further and further into her shell. Her mother, busy with church work, was often away from home.

Then, on one of those days, Susan's father approached her.

"I don't want you hurt again, Susan," he began, "so from now on I will be the one to love you."

Susan was not sure what he meant, but it did not take her long to understand. The incest began that day.

"All good daughters do this with their fathers to show how much they love them," he told her. "I love you more than I love your mother, and you must never tell her or anyone about our love."

Susan felt dirty and ashamed, but escaped into her mind during each episode. The relationship lasted until her father's death, about seven years before I met her.

I have wept for Susan many times in my prayer life. The injustice, torment and misery she has endured surely break the heart of her Lover as well. Susan has been in treatment centers, has tried suicide and has taken scores of different kinds of medication. Since I first met her, she has received professional counseling, and our sweet Lover, Jesus, has given her the release of tears. Slowly she is beginning to trust His love, to experience in small measures its reality. "I can feel it trickle into my heart," she tells me.

Just recently she wrote, "I am forgiving those who have hurt me. I don't blame either of my parents. I forgive them."

I still remind Susan that Jesus loved her all during those terrible years, even when she could not sense His love or presence. He wept for all that was happening to His cherished daughter.

Susan's story may be your story, too. You may have experienced the same kind of suffering and torment. You may be in recovery, or you may never have told a living soul. Jesus will listen. He will weep with you. He has someone who can help you. Dare to trust His love. It is more than sentiment; it is power.

Others reading this chapter cannot imagine the kind of invasion and horror Susan went through, but you have your own disappointments and lost dreams. Jesus weeps for you as well, and cares about your loss. Hold on and never give up. Dare to let Jesus into your world to replace Satan's lies with truths from His Word. Jesus wants to wipe away your tears.

Still others need to hear our Lover's wake-up call to see His devastated creation. As you sit at His feet each day, ask Him to show you where He needs you to be His comforting hands and willing feet. Jesus sees the world's open, gaping sores. He is working on behalf of all those who are hurting, broken and confused. And He is wooing you and me by His Spirit to share His burden and go into fields that are white for harvest, ready for His love and salvation.

His Empathy Never Ends

Anyone who has ever lost a loved one knows the empty feeling that settles in when the funeral is over, the relatives and friends have all gone home, the cards have stopped coming and the bereaved are expected to pick up the threads of their lives as if nothing has happened. Our culture has little patience with sorrow, preferring to pay perfunctory attention and go on its way.

But we have a Lover whose empathy never ends, who will not push us to "get on with life" until He knows we are ready. Recognizing that He weeps with us and for us offers a sweet sense of His abiding intimacy as He fills the voids of our aching places, validating our concerns and affirming our true value. Jesus will weep for you until your healing is complete.

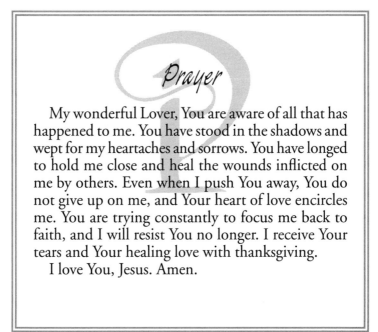

Prayer

My wonderful Lover, You are aware of all that has happened to me. You have stood in the shadows and wept for my heartaches and sorrows. You have longed to hold me close and heal the wounds inflicted on me by others. Even when I push You away, You do not give up on me, and Your heart of love encircles me. You are trying constantly to focus me back to faith, and I will resist You no longer. I receive Your tears and Your healing love with thanksgiving.

I love You, Jesus. Amen.

10

He Is Always on Time

Some time ago I was invited to attend a women's spiritual growth event in which the organizers had invested much thought and prayer. Our nametags had been printed creatively with the weekend theme and with a Scripture chosen individually for each participant. A delightful basket of goodies in each room was filled with more Scripture to ponder. Each woman had been paired with another as a prayer partner for the weekend, and the organizers had set aside time in the schedule for the partners to get acquainted and pray silently for each other.

At one of the group sessions, my prayer partner (I will call her Alicia) favored us with a beautiful praise offering of liturgical dance. We all felt the presence of the Lord as we listened and watched.

Alicia had come to the event, however, with a heavy heart. She was now at an age when dancing was difficult. Through the years her knees and ankles had taken a beating from the constant jumping, bending and moving. Often in pain, she felt hurt and disappointed to realize deep within her spirit that her dancing days were numbered.

Alicia had a close, intimate relationship with her Lover, Jesus—a relationship that was central to her life. But in the area of her life that involved her dancing, her aching place was raw. She loved what she did; it gave her great joy and satisfaction to share her faith in Jesus with the children she taught and with their parents. She also loved to praise Him publicly with her grace and skill.

"It will soon be too late for me to dance," she sighed. "Time has passed and my body has changed."

The question that haunts many women haunted Alicia, too: "Is it too late for me now?" It is a question that nags at modern women as it has nagged women through the ages. Its variations are myriad but its theme is the same: Is it too late to fulfill my dream . . . of marriage, of having a baby, of going back to school, of owning a successful business, of running a marathon, of writing a book, of traveling, of seeing my husband and children come to know Jesus, of serving God in a great and noble way? And as our biological clocks continue to tick, the question stabs deeper and deeper.

It Is *Never* Too Late

Sarai, wife of the great biblical character Abram, was at such a point in her life. Her story is our story, and her God our God.

Some years earlier, God had called Abram and established with him a covenant—a binding agreement common in Middle Eastern culture. In this agreement God had promised Abram land, seed and blessing, and He said that "all the families of the earth" would be blessed through him (Genesis 12:3). The covenant was ratified later, as recorded in Genesis 15, and included the promise of a son for Sarai and Abram, who were childless.

Two chapters later we hear God reiterating the covenant between Himself and Abram and promising a son to Sarai and Abram:

"I will bless her, and indeed I will give you a son by her.
Then I will bless her, and she shall be a mother of nations;
kings of peoples shall come from her."

Genesis 17:16

But this time God added a significant element to the
agreement: He changed Abram's and Sarai's names, which
meant respectively "exalted father" and "my princess," to
"father of a great number" and "princess." God had more
in mind here than just changing the meanings of His friends'
names. To understand His intentions, we need to look at
the covenant-cutting ceremony that surrounded each agreement established in those days between two parties.

Understanding the Ceremony

The ceremony usually took place in an open field with
many witnesses present, and in it each covenantal party
made certain exchanges.

First they exchanged robes to confuse their identities.
People watching from a distance would thereafter be unable
to distinguish one party from the other. Next the covenant-
ing individuals exchanged belts, representing strength, sym-
bolizing their offering of power and strength to each other.
The third exchange involved the weapons hanging on each
party's belt. In essence this stood for the exchanging of enemies: "Your enemy is now my enemy, and my enemy is
yours." Then the two parties exchanged names or underwent a change of names. One person would put the other
person's name in the middle of his own, thus signifying total
identification with the other party. And finally, to conclude
the covenant, the parties always shared a meal.

As God established His covenant with the nomadic shepherd of Middle Eastern background, He understood not
only the ceremony so important in Abram's culture, but its
symbolism as well. So it was that God incorporated His

own name into the middle of Abram's and Sarai's names. It made perfect sense to Abram. He had entered into a covenant with Yahweh, so *Abram* became *Abraham,* with the *ah* from God's name inserted. So, too, was God's *ah* inserted into Sarai's name, for she would play an important part in the covenant.

As a final mark of this agreement, Abraham was circumcised. A man's greatest asset in Middle Eastern society was his ability to procreate, and his greatest curse was infertility. Building a family to care for him and his wife in their old age and to carry on the family line were vital. Thus the circumcision of the male reproductive organ was a powerful outward sign of entering into covenant with God.

Understanding the Middle Eastern covenant ceremony sheds fascinating light on our relationship with God through Jesus. Like Abraham and Sarah, we exchange robes with God: Jesus takes our "robe" of sin on Himself and we are robed in His righteousness. This means we can take on His identity and purpose to be conformed to His image.

We exchange enemies as well. When we receive Christ, Satan becomes our archenemy, and death becomes Jesus' enemy—one He conquered forever when He rose from the dead. God warns us to be aware of Satan's wiles (see 2 Corinthians 2:11), to watch out that he not devour us (see 1 Peter 5:8) and to use God's designated weapons to deal with him (see Ephesians 6:13–18).

Additionally we exchange belts—our belt of weakness for the strength and power of the Holy Spirit that are necessary if we are to live for Him in holiness.

As the final exchange in our covenants, we take Jesus' name: We are called *Christians* and mark the significance of our agreement with the ritual of water baptism. Then we share in the meal Jesus instituted, the Lord's Supper, as we remember our covenant.

"God, About This Baby You Promised . . ."

When it hit Abraham that he would be one hundred years old and Sarah would be ninety by the time they had their baby, he laughed at the prospect. Who could blame him? Then three men visited Abraham, one of whom (it is clear from Genesis 18) was Yahweh in disguise. Sarah overheard their reiteration of God's promise of a child, and the Bible tells us she "laughed to herself, saying, 'After I have become old, shall I have pleasure, my lord being old also?'" (verse 12).

Sarah's laugh was not one of delight or merriment, but of derision and mockery. God heard her, of course, and knew her thoughts, but instead of getting angry, He asked an important question: "Is anything too difficult for the LORD?" (verse 14).

Sarah's story demonstrates the truth that with God it is never too late. Sarah had been promised a child years earlier. Now she was far too old to bear children. How she had longed to hold a baby in her arms and share this joy with her husband! She had been faithful to Abraham, a good wife. But now she had given up hope that the promise would come true. She had even lost her longing. How bittersweet it must have seemed—how laughable, even—for God to say the child would come at this point in her life!

Is It Too Late for You?

Have you ever felt the way Sarah did? Have you looked with anticipation year after year for an answer to a certain prayer that has not come to pass? When our hopes are as sorely tested as Sarah's were, we run the risk of becoming indifferent about our expectations. We no longer feel excited and optimistic about the future. We lose hope and dam up our yearnings.

The following stories of three women illustrate some common circumstances under which we may think it is too late—and forget that our Lover is always on time.

Never Too Late for a Loved One's Salvation

I have talked with many women who once prayed with excitement and anticipation for a mate or child to come to salvation through Jesus. They enlisted the aid of friends at church or Bible study to pray earnestly for that loved one to trust the Lord, or even just to attend church with the family. But week after week, month after month, year after year of patience and prayers and remembering not to nag have brought no response.

These women continue their walks with Jesus, but the ache of not being able to share this wonderful heavenly relationship with one who is humanly close gives way to despair. Many give up inside, their hope diminishing with each passing year. Like the psalmist, they wonder,

> Has [God's] lovingkindness ceased forever? Has His promise come to an end forever? Has God forgotten to be gracious? Or has He in anger withdrawn His compassion?
> Psalm 77:8–9

As we pray faithfully for unsaved loved ones, we need to understand that God will not violate their wills. He will woo them with His love, but they must respond. At the same time, if the psalmist's cry is your cry, let me encourage you not to give up. It is never too late for God to work in someone we love, and nothing is too difficult for Him.

One Sunday morning I overheard a young woman at church say to some peers, "I've been praying for five long years, and have asked others to agree with me in prayer for my husband's salvation, for him to join our family in worship. But my husband is still not saved, and he is still at home!"

Her friends nodded in sympathy, while an older woman standing nearby walked over and put her arm around the young wife.

"My dear," she said, "I prayed 22 long years for my husband to come to faith in Jesus. God has answered, and I want you to know it was worth every minute of the wait."

What a testimony of faith in waiting for God and not giving up on Him!

If you have been struggling with this issue and others surrounding life with an unsaved mate, I recommend Melinda Fish's book *Restoring the Wounded Woman* (Chosen, 1993). But never be like Sarah, laughing bitterly and saying, "It is too late." It is never too late.

Never Too Late for Forgiveness

I received a phone call from Lorraine about six months after I had spoken at her church. We had gotten to know each other only briefly while I was there, but I was delighted to hear her voice. She was composed and articulate, a leader among the women in her congregation. She had been eager that week to sit at the feet of Jesus and soak in all He had to offer.

But Lorraine was not just making a friendly call. She needed help. I listened intently as she told me that her husband, Phil, also a church leader, had begun an affair with a fellow church member.

I run into this problem in churches far more than you would imagine. Our relationship with Jesus does not make us immune to temptation, although Jesus gives us the power to resist and offers us a way of escape (as promised in 1 Corinthians 10:13). But sometimes we fail to heed His warning or take His way out.

That is what happened to Phil. He had been open with Lorraine about the affair but was unwilling to stop seeing the other woman. Both families were involved; both mates knew of the infidelity. It was a mess, and Lorraine was at a loss to know how to respond.

"Are you willing to trust Jesus to see you through this?" I asked her.

"Yes," she replied.

"Are you willing to forgive your husband and seek God's help in restoring the marriage?"

Lorraine hesitated. Finally she answered, "Jan, I think it may be too late for that now."

I understood how Lorraine felt. For most women, unfaithfulness strikes such chords of anger and woundedness that at first they think it is unforgivable. Their self-esteem spirals downward and a sense of betrayal overwhelms them.

From an emotional standpoint, too, it is common for women to feel it is too late for forgiveness and restoration. Infidelity often deals a death blow to the romantic love so foundational (whether rightly or wrongly) to our Western concept of marriage. Without it marriage seems unthinkable.

Lorraine, like many other betrayed women, was struggling with her feelings, especially since Phil was unwilling to withdraw from his illicit relationship. She was not sure she could forgive him even if he did.

I encouraged Lorraine to agree to a prayer covenant. She was to call me frequently so we could talk and pray together about the situation. She knew I would be interceding between our long-distance prayer meetings.

I saw faith begin to blossom with each phone call that followed. I told Lorraine to cling to Jesus, to study His Word and to talk to Him honestly, laying out her pain and allowing His comfort. Although she was a believer, she had never known Him in this intimate way, but she determined to take the time now, regardless of what happened to her marriage.

I began to pray that God would send Lorraine someone in her city to pray with her, encourage her and listen to her confidentially. Jesus answered, and Lorraine was thrilled to have a friend stand by her side. Eventually she became willing to forgive her husband. She decided they had both invested many years in this marriage and that it was worth saving.

Phil, meanwhile, was experiencing confusion and deception—common reactions to infidelity. He was no longer sure he was in love with the other woman, and began to see something winsome and appealing in his wife. He knew she had forgiven him and continued to forgive him every day, but he was still torn by feelings of loyalty to his new relationship.

During this period I had to be out of the area for a long stretch of time. Regretting my inability to talk with Lorraine regularly, I continued praying but wrote down some of my thoughts and mailed them to her. I reminded her of the truths of God about her tangled mess: that because Phil was a believer, he would someday have to account for his behavior, and that it was important for both of us to pray for him to hear the Holy Spirit and obey, to see his own sin and repent.

To my surprise, Lorraine called to tell me she had given my letter to Phil! But God always has His purposes. He used my letter to convict Phil of his adultery, and Lorraine had the privilege of comforting her husband with the fact that Jesus stood ready to forgive. Phil confessed his amazement at her forgiveness, and Lorraine rejected a perfect opportunity to pour salt on his wounds as he sat before her in brokenness.

Lorraine and Phil still have many things to sort out, and have agreed to go to counseling sessions for as long as it takes to restore their marriage. Perhaps years from now they will be used by God to help others realize it is never too late for forgiveness.

Never Too Late to Know Jesus Deeply

While I was preaching a revival in a nearby city one week, I noticed an older woman who came every night and sat in the same place. She never came to the altar at the close of the service to pray, but I saw a look of longing on her face that has become hauntingly familiar in my work with women.

One night she caught up with me after the service and asked if I would talk with her in her car after I had finished talking and praying with others. I agreed, and discovered that, although she had been a church member virtually all her life, she knew something was missing in her Christian experience. That "something" was the intimate fellowship with Jesus that forms the core message of this book.

"The younger women I see are so excited about Jesus," she said wistfully, "and I sense that you are, too. It's too late for me to know Jesus in such a rich, full way, but would you pray with me that the young women in my family could come to know Him like that?"

I am always amazed that anyone could swallow such a huge lie from Satan! Yet some women sincerely feel that a vibrant relationship with the One others know as Lover has passed them by. Since they did not seek Him when they were young, they doubt the offer is still good. They feel set in their ways, unskilled in prayer and Bible study. Such women are saved by Jesus' blood and will go to heaven when they die, but they doubt they can know the rapturous joy that comes from this deeper walk.

Gladly I explained to this dear, yearning woman that it is never too late to know Jesus in a deeply personal and intimate way. There is no age limit to developing a familiar relationship with our Lover. Until we breathe our last, Jesus will continue calling us to closeness with Himself. Until we are no longer able to move, think or respond, He will woo us by His Spirit to a place of in-depth union. Nothing in our past or present can keep us from what He wants to give us, if we will believe Him and dare to move toward Him.

The following evening my new friend came to the altar when the invitation was given, and I was thrilled to pray with her. She drew near to Jesus and He drew near to her. She let Him know she yearned for intimacy with Him, and she asked the Holy Spirit to overflow in her life in a fresh and vital way.

Her encounter with Jesus happened several years ago, and she is still getting closer to her Lover, enjoying His company in a way she never thought possible.

Have you been reading the last several chapters with pain in your heart, thinking it is too late for *you* to make Jesus the Lover you need most? Do not neglect your longing; He has planted it in your heart. Dare to jump into His arms, as Shannon jumped into Dave's, with abandon and trust. He is waiting to hear your voice and touch your heart with hope.

What to Do While You Wait

In the last chapter we mentioned waiting on and for Jesus. Trusting His past record of faithfulness, knowing He works all circumstances together for our good and believing He is interceding for us during times of delay are all pertinent to creative waiting. But the erroneous belief that it is too late for us, too late for our dreams to come true, can erect a wall between us and our Lover, blocking His action on our behalf. In order to tear down that wall, we need to take at least four steps.

1. Be Honest with God

Tired, sad and resigned to her barren lot in life, Sarah determined at some point along the way that it was too late for God to answer her prayers. And for her reaction to God's promise of a son "at this time next year" (Genesis 18:10), she has been vilified in books and sermons.

But to her credit, Sarah was being honest with Him. "After I have become old," she laughed, "shall I have pleasure, my lord being old also?" (Genesis 18:12). I think she was saying, in essence, "Oh, right. Now that Abraham and I are too old to enjoy a sexual experience, with all its closeness, God is coming through with His promise. This is laughable. It's obviously too late for a son!"

Sarah was blurting out, in the solitude of her tent, what she was really thinking and feeling. She was wrong about what God could and would do, but at least she was honest.

Have you ever wanted to say to God, "It's too late now! You've come with too little, too late." He already sees our thoughts and knows our hearts. Our honesty will not offend Him, and it is healthier than silent resignation or sublimated bitterness and despair.

Do you trust your Lover enough to reveal even this aching place to Him? Cry it out to Him. He is able to listen, to understand, to comfort you and lead you to higher ground.

2. Examine Your Motives

In her book *Adventures in Prayer,* Catherine Marshall noted an obvious danger for the Christian asking God to answer a prayer: Does my request spring from my selfish human will or from God's will? Remember James' warning to the Jewish Christians: "You ask and do not receive, because you ask with wrong motives, so that you may spend it on your pleasures" (James 4:3).

Catherine Marshall suggested we ask ourselves several questions that are a good test of the motives behind any request:

- Will my dream fulfill the talents, temperament and emotional needs God has planted in my being? This is not easy to answer. It involves knowing yourself, the real person, as few of us do.
- Does my dream involve taking anything or any person belonging to someone else? Would its fulfillment

hurt another human being? If so, you can be fairly sure this particular dream is not God's will for you.

- Am I willing to make all my relationships with other people right? If I hold resentments, grudges, bitterness, these wrong emotions, no matter how "justified," will cut me off from God, the source of creativity. Furthermore, no dream can be achieved in a vacuum of human relationships. Even one such wrong relationship can cut the channel of God's power.
- Do I want this dream with my whole heart? Dreams are not usually brought to fruition in divided personalities; only the whole heart is willing to do its part toward implementing the dream.
- Am I willing to wait patiently for God's timing?
- Am I dreaming big? The bigger the dream and the more persons it will benefit, the more apt it is to stem from the infinite designs of God.

To these questions, I would ask another, paraphrased from Marshall's insightful book on prayer:

- Am I willing to relinquish my request, taking my own will out of the way, so that God can move in the way He deems best?

3. Search God's Word

An additional "check and balance" to assure ourselves that we are praying and dreaming with the right motivation is developing a good grasp of the great principles and promises of God's Word. Catherine Marshall noted that if our request would harm any other human being, it is contrary to God's will. The operative biblical principles would be the commandments not to take or covet anything that is our neighbor's (see Exodus 20:15, 17) and to love our neighbors as we love ourselves (see Leviticus 19:18).

So while you are waiting for God to act in a particular area of your life, spend your time creatively by searching and learning God's Word. Have a larger goal than simply finding promises that fit your situation. Sit at His feet as you study, allowing Him to teach you about Himself, about His "big picture" and about refinements He wants to make in you. Often God must do a work in us before we are ready to receive His answer to our request.

I believe God had to change Sarah's heart before Isaac, the long-promised baby, could be born. She needed to be emptied of her sourness and to forgive many people, including herself. She needed to learn to wait for God, because an even greater test lay ahead, when Abraham would be asked to take their only son to Mount Moriah and offer him back as a sacrifice to the very One who had given him in the first place.

We are not told whether Sarah knew, prior to Abraham and Isaac's early morning departure for Mount Moriah, what their mission was (see Genesis 22:3). But that is almost irrelevant. Waiting while knowing the test of faith Abraham was undergoing would have been agonizing. But waiting *without* knowing, wondering what her husband and son were doing and being forced to trust Abraham's integrity and her own knowledge of God's past dealings with their family, would have been, for most women, equally hard. Regardless of what she knew, I think Sarah must have waited in a different way on that occasion, believing it is never too late for God to fulfill His promises. I doubt she was too surprised when Isaac and his father came home safe and sound to share the miracle of God's provision of an alternate sacrifice (see Genesis 22:13). Perhaps Sarah smiled inside, amazed at her own composure and realizing how deeply she had come to trust Yahweh.

It is the same with us. When we take time to sit at the feet of Jesus and learn our lessons from His Word and

His Holy Spirit, each test builds more faith for the next one.

4. Never Try to "Help" God

You probably recall that in Sarah's despair and eagerness for God's promise to be fulfilled, she had decided to take things into her own hands. She thought she would help God out. So when she was in her late seventies or eighties, Sarah followed an accepted custom of her culture and gave her maidservant Hagar to Abraham as a concubine, hoping a son would come from the union (see Genesis 16:2).

One did, whom Abraham named Ishmael. Both Abraham and Sarah assumed this boy to be the promised heir. But this was not God's plan, even though, legally speaking—since Hagar belonged to Sarah—the child could have been considered Sarah's.

No, Ishmael was not the son God promised. He was the result of Sarah's attempt to fulfill her longings (and, incidentally, God's promise) in her own way. The arrangement brought grief to the whole family. Hagar, proud of her accomplishment, looked down on her childless mistress. Sarah allowed resentment to take root in her heart, coming to hate both Hagar and Ishmael and actually conspiring to banish them from her sight—not once but twice. Abraham, of course, was caught miserably in the middle.

When we take things out of God's hands and into our own, we often create immense problems that only muddy the waters of our circumstances. "Assisting" God puts us on dangerous ground. Instead of being problem-solvers, we become part of the problem, and usually end up interfering with and actually delaying God's plan.

A good friend of mine discovered this hard-to-swallow truth when the younger of her two daughters began to rebel in her teenage years. I talked with my friend countless times; we prayed and sought God's wisdom and will. But each time her daughter got into trouble, my friend was there to bail her out. When the girl made empty promises to change, Mom offered money without waiting to see if the changes were sincere. Again and again she swooped in as savior, and again and again endured self-doubt, guilt, broken promises and the fear that her daughter was lost for good.

Throughout this difficult time, I encouraged my friend to stop rescuing her daughter, since rescuing delays God's intervention in our older children's lives. There is a difference between temporary acts of family kindness for an isolated need or two, and a pattern of enabling a child to keep rebelling without consequences. When we parents lose our perspective in this area and try to become our children's savior, they have no motivation to seek the one, true Savior, Jesus Christ.

But my friend, like many parents, felt her rescues assured the child of her love. She was afraid of conveying the message "I don't care what happens to you."

The truth is, at a certain point, our children must face the results of their own behavior and choices. Our refusal to rescue offers a much deeper love, because the longer we insist on habitually rescuing our kids, the longer it will take for them to become spiritually, mentally and emotionally whole.

After years of rescuing her daughter, my friend finally listened as the Holy Spirit taught her that, like Sarah, she had been trying to help God out. In a recent conversation she told me, "I won't rescue her any longer, Jan. I'm done with that!"

I was thrilled and hopeful. I know Jesus loves her daughter, and now my friend is freeing Him to help her child come to the end of her own financial and emotional resources—indeed, to the end of herself. While continuing to offer prayer and moral support, my friend can allow God to take charge of the situation.

When we make the mistake of "helping" God, we only prolong our wait for His wonderful answer to our need.

Our Lover Is Always on Time

Once we have trusted Jesus and His promises, we must not get comfortable again with unbelief. Sarah adjusted to her barrenness and, even though she complained about it, accepted it as a normal pattern in her life.

We can get so comfortable with the dysfunction in our own lives and those of our families that we stop seeking answers from our Lover. We can grow accustomed to our hang-ups and fail to ask for forgiveness and deliverance. We get so discouraged waiting for God to act that unbelief becomes a lifestyle. Deep in our spirits we think it is too late, and we live out this belief in our thoughts, words and actions.

My friend Alicia, the dancer, sought her Lover during the weekend we spent at that women's retreat. She laid before His throne the realization that her days for dancing and teaching little ones to dance were over, and she told Him she was willing to be His handmaiden in whatever role He had for her now. She had faith that it was not too late for Him to accomplish His purposes in her life at this new stage.

Today Alicia offers her vast know-how to other dancers who teach dancing. She tells me that, as a consultant, she finds many more doors open to her in sharing her faith in her Lover than she experienced before. Beautiful and confident, she is trusting Jesus to prosper this new adventure.

It is never too late for us when we belong to Jesus Christ— never too late for our Lover to show us new direction and purpose. It is never too late for Him to fulfill His promises in our lives and in the lives of those we love. In fact, He is right on time.

What "impossible" thing do you long for? Will it glorify Jesus? Have you searched His Word? Lay your dreams before Him. He is waiting to hold you and impart hope. Our Lover is always on time.

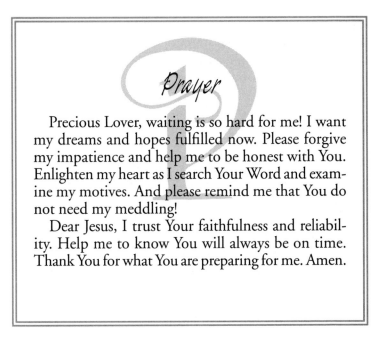

Prayer

Precious Lover, waiting is so hard for me! I want my dreams and hopes fulfilled now. Please forgive my impatience and help me to be honest with You. Enlighten my heart as I search Your Word and examine my motives. And please remind me that You do not need my meddling!

Dear Jesus, I trust Your faithfulness and reliability. Help me to know You will always be on time. Thank You for what You are preparing for me. Amen.

Part 3

LOVING THE ONE WHO LOVES YOU

11

Loving through Praise

In chapter 5 we talked about Leah, who learned after many years to trust God to be her Lover and source of self-esteem. Her story of insecurity and insignificance—and of renewed inner strength and purpose—can be our story as well. But the account of Leah shows another wonderful nugget of truth to us as we talk about allowing Jesus to be our ultimate Lover. Leah learned not only how to take from her Lover, but one important way in which she could give to Him and love Him back.

Remember that Leah had four sons, each of whose names represented to some degree her emotional state when he was born. The first three were born when Leah was struggling mightily in her relationships with her husband, her sister, herself and God. But Leah named her last son Judah, which means "praise" or "praise the Lord." Her complete statement in Genesis 29:35 was, "This time I will praise the Lord." What did she mean?

Leah's words were definitely a declaration of intent to change her pattern of seeking self-esteem through her husband, her children and her accomplishments. She finally saw that only her Lover, God, could be her complete and flawless source of self-esteem.

But Leah's statement had deeper meaning. I believe her discovery of God as her Lover, and her new understanding of what His cherishing would mean, made her decide to give Him the honor and exultation of her soul through praise.

What Is Praise?

If you are a new believer in Jesus and have only just begun to participate in the family of God, the word *praise* may sound churchy and old-fashioned. "Praise the Lord" may be a phrase you have heard used by people you thought were fanatics, and it gives you a funny feeling. Just what is this thing called praise?

Even if you have been a Christian for a long time, you still may not know what praise really is. Perhaps it is one of those "Christianese" buzzwords you adopted from your parents or someone at church, but were never sure what it meant or how to do it. Time has gone by and everyone assumes you "get it," so you feel embarrassed to admit your ignorance.

In either case, you are part of a large crowd within the Body of Christ! Very few Christians truly understand what it means to praise God, much less what our praise means to God. So if we are to make praise a way we love our Lover, we need to examine both the word *praise* and what the Bible tells us about it.

The American Heritage Dictionary defines *praise* as "an expression of warm approval or admiration; strong commendation." The Bible is clear that God wants our warm approval and admiration! In fact, Psalm 22:3 tells us that He lives in, or is "enthroned upon," the praises of His people. The songwriter David frequently enjoined the Israelites (and us, their spiritual descendants) to offer praise to God. "Make His praise glorious," he said in Psalm 66:2. Another exhortation of David—"Enter . . . His courts with praise" (Psalm 100:4)—identifies praise as the means to enter God's presence. (More on that later.) David himself, who had a close friendship with God, had learned that it was "good to sing praises to our God" (Psalm 147:1).

Praise Delights the Heart of God

David also made the interesting comment that praise "is becoming to the upright" (Psalm 33:1; see also Psalm 147:1). Praise makes us good-looking in God's sight! And, of course, that gives Him delight.

Countless biblical figures made praising God a standard of their lives, and delighted the Almighty in the process. Moses, the acclaimed deliverer of God's people from Egypt, burst into praise when God brought the masses safely through the Red Sea on dry land and the Pharaoh was defeated: "The LORD is my strength and song, and He has become my salvation. This is my God, and I will praise Him; my father's God, and I will extol Him" (Exodus 15:2). Moses' sister, Miriam, grabbed a timbrel and sang out, "Sing to the LORD, for He is highly exalted; the horse and his rider He has hurled into the sea" (verse 21).

Even though Daniel, as a captive outsider in Babylon, was in a precarious situation, he never stopped praising the God who had shown Himself faithful. Jeremiah and Joel, too, spoke of a future time of restoration for God's chosen people, when they would again praise God and honor Him with pure hearts.

Jesus added to the wealth of biblical references about praise when He quoted Psalm 8:2: "From the mouths of children and babies I'll furnish a place of praise" (Matthew 21:16, TM). God so desires praise that He will make it happen! And Luke 10:21 notes that Jesus "rejoiced greatly in the Holy Spirit." The word picture from the original Greek suggests that He leaped about in exuberance! Praise may be quiet or ebullient, private or public.

In Acts 16 we read the story of Paul and Silas praising God from a cell in the Philippian jail. Apparently they were not praising God silently, because verse 25 tells us "the prisoners were listening to them." In fact, they may have been raising the roof!

Praise to God: glorious, good-looking, exuberant, joyful, sometimes quiet and sometimes loud. How could we *not* want to please our Lover by letting Him know we think He is great?

Praise Keeps Our Eyes on Jesus Despite the Circumstances

A likable, bubbly young woman named Dale, at whose wedding I sang and played my guitar, called me frantically one day to tell me the result of a biopsy: a previously discovered lump in her breast was malignant.

I had watched Dale grow spiritually in a Sunday school class I led, and enjoyed her childlike, determined walk with Jesus. With each year of maturity, by the power of the Holy Spirit, she had made Jesus the Lover of her life on a deeper level. Now she was asking for my prayers.

Dale loved to praise Jesus, whether at home, in her car with praise tapes or at church with her Christian family. In this crisis she refused to allow anything to diminish her desire to give God her approval and admiration. Every now and then she phoned me to say, "Jan, I must get together with others and praise Jesus." It reminded me of David in Psalm 22:22: "In the midst of the assembly I will praise Thee."

So Dale, her husband and I and several other Christians would gather around the altar of our sanctuary, turn the lights down low and worship and praise our Lover. God never failed to come and inhabit those times of adoration. We saw in a marvelous way how such corporate praise brought deep joy and peace, not only to Dale in her crisis, but to the rest of us as well.

What Dale learned through our worship gatherings was that praising Jesus kept her eyes on Him. As we met together, her faith was boosted, her husband was strengthened and they were enabled to continue on their difficult journey. All of us who joined Dale in praise—and later in thanksgiving as she went into remission—found that our eyes went from the tragedy of cancer to the love of the One who would never fail us, who was there to hold us close. We gained a new joy in belonging to Him, and to the reality of being connected to, and keeping our eyes on, the right Source.

Praise Helps Us Grasp the Infinite

Praise has a way of transcending the present and putting us into the heavenly realms. Ephesians 2:6 tells us that our standing with God through our relationship with His Son has "seated us with Him in the heavenly places, in Christ Jesus." Theologians call this the *positional* reality of our faith, meaning that regardless of how we feel, being seated with Christ in the heavenlies is without dispute part of our inheritance as Christians, the result of Jesus' death on the cross.

But it means more. I believe that, with the help of the Holy Spirit, we can begin to experience the heavenly realms now, while we are still on earth. We capture this foretaste in many ways, and praise is one of the most glorious. True praise gives us a continuing appreciation of the infinite and sovereign God we adore. It puts us into a fuller fusion with the reality of His power and majesty.

My friend Dale experienced this. A few years after her first sad phone call, we learned that cancer had struck again. Eventually it would take her life. But as she had done before, Dale persisted in admiring and adoring her Lover. We had many touching conversations concerning the intimate things He showed her as she praised and worshiped Him every day. His voice became clear to her. His encouragement to her was endless, offering deep ministry to her aching place. She was in love with Him in a way only another person in love can understand, and it bridged the gap between the awful pain in her life and the reality of the infinite God who is beyond the limitations of time and space.

I believe that when Dale saw Jesus face to face, it was not her first glimpse of her Lover. She had already seen and known Him in the heavenly realms through praise.

Praise Is an Attitude

Praise is an attitude of the heart and mind. It catches us up in the wonder and awesomeness of God. It helps change our thought patterns and it gets our eyes back on the One who is able to do all things. An attitude of praise always restores a right perspective on life. Praise breaks the grip of despair in which our failed dreams, bondage, loss of self-esteem and mixed-up priorities have held us. The result: a new trust and reliance on our Lover and His ability to be our all in all.

Attitudes do not develop instantaneously; they must be cultivated. It is easy to tell from reading Paul's letters in the New Testament that he lived in an attitude of praise. (That is why praise seemed the normal thing to do, even in a Philippian jail!)

Dale lived in an attitude of praise, too, and her Lover honored her for it, enabling her to rise above the ravages of disease and early death to bless others within her reach. Once, while she was going through chemotherapy, she found out I was having a bout with my back, and she sent over a casserole. I marveled at her ability to care about others when she, too, was hurting.

The Sunday before Dale died, I was in her home to serve her holy Communion. She could barely swallow the elements and could not talk at all. Yet she squeezed my hand and smiled at me when I prayed for her. I was transfixed by her countenance and by the glow around her. She was enveloped in the love of Jesus, and her decision to make praising Him a life attitude was evident to the end.

Praise Releases the Power of God

Look again at the story of Paul and Silas in jail. Most of us would have been praying for deliverance from our imprisonment, or complaining because God had allowed it in the first place. Instead Paul and Silas praised God with gusto, and the whole building began to shake. The prisoners' chains were loosened and all the jail doors opened. Paul and Silas were led out by a courtesy escort, and late that night the jailer on duty and all his family received Christ.

It is a fact: Praise releases the power of God in ways we might never have imagined. That is not *why* we praise; we praise because it gives pleasure to our Lover to see us focus on Him and not on our problems. But since God will never violate our free wills or push His way into our lives, the very act of praise tells Him we are taking our hands off our circumstances and giving Him permission to handle our needs in His own, infinitely better way.

Praise Routs the Enemy

This is a close corollary to the last principle. One of the most exciting examples of its truth took place when King Jehoshaphat of Judah was faced with a great enemy army come to make war. "Jehoshaphat was afraid" (2 Chronicles 20:3). But rather than pick up the hotline to put his armies on alert, he gathered all his subjects and proceeded to expound on the greatness of God and His past faithfulness in dealing with the Israelites. The Bible says the Holy Spirit fell on a young man, who gave the word of encouragement Jehoshaphat had been hoping for:

> "Do not fear or be dismayed because of this great multitude, for the battle is not yours but God's. Tomorrow go down against [the enemy]. . . . You need not fight in this battle; station yourselves, stand and see the salvation of the

LORD on your behalf, O Judah and Jerusalem. Do not fear
or be dismayed; tomorrow go out to face them, for the
LORD is with you."

2 Chronicles 20:15–17

At this point not only did everyone believe the words
were from God, but they demonstrated their confidence—
by praising, thanking and worshiping Him—that His
promise would come true:

And Jehoshaphat bowed his head with his face to the
ground, and all Judah and the inhabitants of Jerusalem fell
down before the LORD, worshiping the LORD. And the
Levites . . . stood up to praise the LORD God of Israel, with
a very loud voice.

verses 18–19

It was an astounding reaction, humanly speaking, when
you realize what they were up against. Still, what happened
next is the best part of the story. The following day, before
the battle, King Jehoshaphat

consulted with the people [and] appointed those who sang
to the LORD and those who praised Him in holy attire, as
they went out before the army and said, "Give thanks to
the LORD, for His lovingkindness is everlasting."

verse 21

It must have been quite a sight to see the praise choir out
there in front of the soldiers, marching toward the enemy,
singing and praising with all their might! God honored their
praise and obedience:

When they began singing and praising, the LORD set
ambushes against the sons of Ammon, Moab, and Mount
Seir, who had come against Judah; so they were routed. For
the sons of Ammon and Moab rose up against the inhab-

itants of Mount Seir destroying them completely, and when
they had finished with the inhabitants of Seir, they helped
to destroy one another.

verses 22–23

God, honoring the Israelites' confidence, threw the enemy
soldiers into such confusion that they ended up killing one
another. Just as God had promised, the Israelites did not
have to fight, and their nation was saved.

Sometimes the attacks of the enemy are not so blatant.
Often at the close of a revival or conference, or even at the
end of a day at home, I feel drained and lifeless. Many stories I hear break my heart—stories of shattered relationships, unfulfilled promises, people's unwillingness to allow
Jesus to intervene in their lives and bring them back to
wholeness. I answer letter after letter from godly women
pleading passionately for prayer to sustain them in the pain
and heartache they are experiencing. I listen, counsel and
do my best to help by God's grace, but I recognize the need
to roll these burdens over to Jesus before the evening ends
so that Satan does not overwhelm me with the sorrows of
the world.

I can stand in faith with people and commit their every
need to prayer. I can believe God's promises with them. I
can elaborate on the riches of His Word to their spirits. But
I cannot hold onto their burdens.

What do I do? Go to my room, pick up my guitar and
climb into the middle of my bed. Then I begin to praise
and worship the Lover of my life, sometimes in soft hymns
or choruses of adoration, sometimes in loud, robust songs
of power and victory. He is the One who has all power and
wisdom to meet every need. He is the One who sees the
end from the beginning and has a plan for each life that has
touched mine that day. I get in touch with Him and receive
His soothing ointment for my aching place.

I need the renewal that comes from praise. When I focus on praising His greatness, majesty and love, I feel a trickle of His power and presence with me, encircling me with the splendor and beauty of His holiness. I can release the burdens of all I have seen and heard to Him, knowing that in this time of praise and worship, I am offering intercession for them on a level deeper than my words could ever convey. Praise has brought me peace and release. I am no longer drained and vulnerable to the enemy. I am filled with the presence of Jesus.

The truth of this praise principle cannot be overtaught or overpreached. When we belong to Jesus Christ and have made Him our Source, the battles are His, not ours. Praise routs the enemy. It did so in the time of ancient Israel, and it does so now.

Different Kinds of Praise

Many people are not aware that the words *praise* or *bless* or *glory* in Scripture carry different meanings and purposes. Often we translate a word as *praise* that has a variant meaning. The word *barak,* for example, means a form of praise that carries with it reverence, adoration and blessing of God in a deep, often quiet way. Psalm 100:4 uses this specific word: "Enter His gates with thanksgiving, and His courts with praise." This form of praise is probably most familiar to us. (In fact, many of us know only this form of praise.) We come into the house of God with reverent praise. Often in our own devotional times, we come quietly in honor of His name.

Another Hebrew word for praise, *shachah,* means to bow down or to stoop in worship. This is a kneeling form of praise. When we go to the altar at church, we are praising God in this way. In 2 Chronicles 20:18, where King Jehoshaphat bowed his head with his face to the ground and worshiped God, it is this word that is used. He was humbling himself before the Lord, as we do when we kneel.

If I took a survey of most Christians, these two forms of worship would be the ones most often used. We know God is holy, and we want to enter His presence and praise Him in awe and reverence. And sometimes we feel the need to bow down or kneel before Him. But there are other words that mean to praise or bless or bring glory to God that we may not know.

The Hebrew word *shabach* means to praise in a loud tone and to acclaim loudly His glory. This is praise that pleases God, too. There are times we should kneel or come quietly to praise our King, and there are times to shout His excellence and greatness!

The word *zamar* means to praise God with instruments. This, too, is pleasing to the Lord. On Sunday mornings when we gather in church, the prelude means much more than just having music while we get seated. It is a form of praise to God with an instrument, and it is designed so that we can focus on the Lord and prepare our hearts to worship Him aright. Psalm 150 uses this expression as it speaks of praising God with the trumpet, harp, stringed instruments, pipes and cymbals. All these and many more are dedicated to giving glory to God and honoring His name.

Some people are familiar with the word *halal,* which is also a word for praise. We get our English word *Hallelujah* from it. It means to boast, make a show, even be foolish in our adoration! Have you ever heard someone shout, "Hallelujah!" when the pastor exalted God with a point in his sermon? Some people might be embarrassed by this outburst, but if it is from a heart of praise, a heart filled with joyful agreement, then God is pleased and blessed. Second Chronicles 20:19 uses this word when it says that the Levites rose up to praise the God of Israel with loud voices.

The word *thillah* is close in meaning to *halal*. It, too, means to laud, boast or rave about the Lord. Isn't it wonderful that we can rave about our great God and Savior?

Other words used in the Bible show different expressions of praise. One more is *yadah,* which means to praise God with extended hands, or hands open; and it implies confession or acknowledgment. When you stand to give God a testimony from your own heart and experience, this is the kind of praise you offer Him. Or if you ever raise a hand during worship, or open your palms to express love or reverence, this is *yadah* worship. It is this final example that was used in Genesis 29:35 when Leah made her declaration before God. She may have lifted her hand to the heavens when she made this statement of confession and acknowledgment, or not. But the word *praise* here means to acknowledge. How fitting! Leah had decided to praise the Lord. It was a decision, a confession and an acknowledgment of making Him her Source.

Six Ways to "Practice" Praise

Praise is included in our Sunday morning worship services not to fill up time or pep us up before the sermon. It is the foremost reason we are gathered in the first place. The praise and worship of our great King and Savior stands alone. We have come into His house to honor and glorify His name.

It is the same in our times of private worship, when we choose the better part and sit at Jesus' feet. When we praise and worship with our whole beings, thinking about the object of our affection, allowing worship to wash away the worries of the day, extolling Him in our hearts, we become more receptive to His voice. He engulfs us in His great presence as we surrender ourselves in praise.

Jesus told the woman at the well that "true worshipers shall worship the Father in spirit and truth; for such people the Father seeks to be His worshipers" (John 4:23). God wants us to worship with abandoned joy and undivided hearts, with pure motives and a longing to honor Him.

Do you need a more concentrated life of praise to your Lover? When you are first learning how to praise Him, it may help to "practice" in your own quiet times with Him. Once you are comfortable praising Him there, you will be able to do so anywhere. Here are six ways to make it happen.

1. Clear Away Hindrances

Ask your Lover to help you clear away any hindrances. Obstacles can prevent your times of praise from pleasing your Lover and giving you joy. These obstacles include:

A lack of priority. Be sure your will is fully engaged as you praise. Deliberately set aside your Day-Timer, the morning news or whatever else might hinder quality time with Jesus.

Unconfessed sin. Unconfessed sin does not just go away; it blocks our fellowship and oneness with Jesus. We can rationalize, excuse and deny, but only confession brings forgiveness and a clear path of communication between ourselves and our Lover. Failure to confess sin will turn your praise and adoration into futile acts. If you are not sure whether something is hindering your fellowship with Him, ask the Holy Spirit to point out any subtle sins of attitude or willfulness. His word to you will touch on specific wrongdoing; it will not come as vague, nagging guilt.

An unsurrendered heart. Our life with Jesus begins with one big surrender when we accept Him into our lives, but it continues with daily surrenders as we allow Him to be Lord. Fill your heart and thoughts with Him every day and ask the Holy Spirit to search out any ways in which your surrender has been divided or compromised.

Satan's opposition. We must remember constantly that we are in spiritual warfare when we belong to Jesus. Satan often uses distraction or discouragement to pull us away from time with our Lover. We need to be aware of his tactics and be willing to submit ourselves to God and resist the enemy (see James 4:7). Remember, we have authority in the name of Jesus to tell our enemy to be gone.

Constant interruptions. Try to pick a time and place where you know you can spend uninterrupted time with your Lover. Take the phone off the hook, and if your mind keeps drifting to things you need to do, jot them down so you will no longer think about them. When interruptions come, do not allow them to pull you away completely. Be persistent.

Lack of expectancy. Do not come hesitantly into God's presence, thinking this time of praise will be boring. Come expecting to enjoy your time with Jesus. And expect Him to enjoy being with you.

2. Be Silent before Him

Once all the hindrances are gone, come into Jesus' presence quietly. Do not speak; instead, think about His beauty and loveliness, and let Him touch your spirit. Praise music may help you focus, but allow for some times of complete silence.

3. Express Your Affection

Tell your Lover how you feel about Him. Never be afraid to lavish on Him your affection. Think about a human being you love deeply—a spouse, a child, a grandmother. In what ways does it feel natural for you to express your feelings toward that person? Now use some of those same, familiar expressions to begin praising Jesus.

4. Think about His Greatness

Let the Holy Spirit help you think about your Lover's greatness. Meditate on a biblical passage about His majesty,

His power or some great action He has taken on behalf of a Bible character, or on your behalf. There is no need to rush; absorb each truth and give thanks purposefully for who He is and all He has done for you.

5. Take Praise Breaks

Think about Him throughout your day and remind yourself of His presence. Sing a song to Him on your way to work or as you clean your house or care for your children. Share His praises with your little ones, talking to them naturally about His goodness and the things He does to make our world a wonderful place. You will be not only practicing praise yourself, but teaching them that praise can come from our thoughts, our lips or our service to Jesus. It becomes intertwined with who we are.

6. Spend a Day with Jesus

Finally, as you grow more comfortable in praising Jesus, set aside a day and spend it with Him. For this day I offer some suggestions:

Assume that God has not forgotten all your needs and the needs of those for whom you are interceding. Release them to Him and approach Him only with praise; make no requests except for His presence and companionship.

You may want to begin by thanking Him for all He has done for you, and then move into praise. Psalm 100:4 says we are to "enter His gates with thanksgiving, and His courts with praise." This gives us a word picture of Solomon's Temple, with the gates in the outer walls but the courts closer in, nearer to the Holy of Holies. Do you see? We are to enter His presence with thanksgiving, but venture deep into His courts, closer to His heart, with praise. We can usually think of plenty of things to thank Jesus for, but praise goes deeper into who He is, focusing on His nature,

His majesty and His worth. Fix your spirit on His glory and splendor. Bring His attributes or character traits to mind, and let each one bring you into a deeper understanding of His love for you.

A day apart with Jesus will help catch you up in the truth that your great Lover, the Maker of the universe, the omnipotent Ruler of the heavens, loves you and enjoys being with you. You can dare to praise Him with your whole heart, for He will reveal to you that He is more than capable of being all you will ever need. Jesus, your Lover, is enough. Let your joy and spirit soar!

Learning How to Praise Gets Us Ready for Heaven

One day we will join the throngs of heaven who are bowed in praise, surrender and worship. If we have learned how to praise our Lover here, we will feel right at home. Praise in heaven will be a perfect extension of what we began with Him during our lives on earth.

Even now, as we realize our completeness in Him alone and make Him our praise, we can understand the magnitude of our Lover's glory as proclaimed in these words from Psalm 113:1–3:

> Praise the LORD! Praise, O servants of the LORD. Praise the name of the LORD. Blessed be the name of the LORD from this time forth and forever. From the rising of the sun to its setting, the name of the LORD is to be praised.

In the next chapter, let's look at further ways to love our Lover.

Prayer

Precious Jesus, my Lover and Redeemer, I exalt Your holy name. I overflow with cascading waves of gratitude and adoration. Your grace and mercy overwhelm me, and Your might and power stir my soul. I belong to the Creator of the universe, and in You my life finds meaning.

How I praise You, Lord! I worship You with all that is within me. Let my hymn of praise bless You, O Holy One. May my worship please Your heart and connect me to You in a more profound way. I love You more than words can say. Amen.

12

Loving through Spiritual Disciplines

Jeanette was an adult when she gave her life to Jesus. I had the privilege of praying with her the day she began her journey with her Lover. She told me she had been waiting for this kind of relationship all her life! Jeanette embraced Jesus with all her being and determined to make her walk with Him her top priority. Whenever I saw Jeanette and her husband, I could tell she was growing more and more in love with Jesus.

Then, several years after she came to know Jesus, she experienced a trial that could have defeated her faith. It came one evening in the form of a numbing phone call. Jeanette's sister, who lived in a large northern city and for whom Jeanette prayed faithfully, had been murdered, apparently by her live-in boyfriend. They had been high on drugs at the time, and the police had the boyfriend in custody. Jeanette was asked to come and identify her sister's body.

Reporting to the city morgue to see the remains of a loved one after a violent death is an unspeakable trauma. But after Jeanette cared for the necessary details, she sought out the authorities, expressing her concern about the young man who had committed the murder and asking if she could see him. They were surprised she cared but would not grant her request.

So Jeanette returned home, where she and her husband began to pray for the killer. They asked Jesus to help Jeanette construct a letter to let the young man know she had forgiven him. The final draft also included her own testimony of faith in Jesus.

Amazingly Jeanette formed a friendship with the young man. Letters flowed back and forth. Jeanette was able to send a Bible to his jail cell. Eventually she and her husband had the joy of leading the young man to salvation through Jesus Christ. Although he had been sentenced to life in prison, he now had the hope of Jesus within.

Jeanette had gone deeply into the union with Jesus she so willingly sought. As a result of making Jesus her Lover, she had no room for resentment or bitterness. When the crisis came, those emotions had been washed away and replaced with a light in her eye and joy on her face. Molded daily into the image of her Savior, she was able to show her sister's killer the mercy, forgiveness, care and self-sacrifice Jesus had shown her. And that made all the difference in the world to the one person she had every right, humanly speaking, to despise. Her vulnerability to the love of Jesus had changed her profoundly.

Loving Our Lover Takes Determination and Discipline

If we are to meet the daily grind as well as crises of our lives with Jesus' grace, peace and love, we need (as I said in chapter 8) to be sitting at His feet with regularity, so that our Lover's personality becomes intertwined with our own. As in any relationship, getting and staying close to Jesus take the determination to invest time and effort. We need to be so committed to Him that this relationship comes first, no matter what. Then we will find many ways to draw near, knowing He will draw near to us as well.

Making an intimate relationship with Jesus our top priority takes not only determination but discipline. Many other things—most of them admirable, some of them not—will vie for our attention. But there are no shortcuts to a strong, tender relationship with our Lover.

We also discussed in chapter 8 some steps toward learning to sit at the feet of Jesus: making an initial evaluation of our relationship with Him; learning to tarry in His presence; and developing ways to sense His presence so we feel comfortable talking with Him. In this chapter let's go a bit farther, discussing some activities that can help us love our Lover more deeply still as we sit at His feet. These activities are commonly called "spiritual disciplines," but they do not imply grim duty, much less punishment. They simply require our wholehearted determination and willingness, assisted by the Holy Spirit, to corral our God-given energies and focus our minds to be with Jesus.

Five Spiritual Disciplines to Help You Love Your Lover

Jesus, the Lover we need so desperately, has changed the lives of women down through the ages—women in biblical times, women in medieval times, women in Renaissance times, women on every continent, women in the modern world. He is the One we have always longed for, and He alone offers the union with almighty God that puts us on the path to healing for our aching place, and wholeness for our bodies, minds and spirits.

In order to appropriate that healing and wholeness—and, beyond that, to express to our Lover our devotion and joy in Him—let's explore five spiritual disciplines that have come down to us through the ages. They are:

1. Bible Study

If you were in love with a poet or writer, you would want to read his works in order to understand his inner thoughts and dreams. If you were in love with an artist, a racecar driver or a sportsman, you would ask questions and visit the places he loves—in short, you would try to find out all you could about what motivates and pleases him.

So it is that, if our intimate relationship with Christ is to deepen, we cannot neglect the Word of God. There we discover the vital life He has planned for us when we come to Jesus as Savior and Lover. We learn to know His thoughts, His values, His principles, His character and the ways in which we are to behave as citizens of His Kingdom. Through His Word we come to realize the benefits and privileges of our position as His daughters. We receive assurances of His love, protection, cleansing, instruction and provision.

The Bible is like no other book. Hebrews 4:12 says:

> The word of God is living and active and sharper than any two-edged sword, and piercing as far as the division of soul and spirit, of both joints and marrow, and able to judge the thoughts and intentions of the heart.

Colossians 3:16 says, "Let the word of Christ richly dwell within you." From Jesus' own prayer to His Father, we know we are sanctified, or set apart, by way of the Word: "Sanctify them in the truth; Thy Word is truth" (John 17:17). And God said: "My word . . . which goes forth from My mouth . . . shall not return to Me empty, without accomplishing what I desire, and without succeeding in the matter for which I sent it" (Isaiah 55:11). God's Word always has a purpose, and He sees to it that His purpose is completed.

We know from the Parable of the Sower in Luke 8 that Satan wants to steal God's Word from us. It may look as though Satan is trying to hurt us through circumstances or finances or in some other way, but his great desire is to steal the Word of God from us so we are left depleted. Part of the discipline that pleases our Lover is our determination not to let circumstances or lack of planning rob us of time in His Word.

Years ago many Christians memorized Scripture; this is still a good practice today. Many times I have found the Word of God on my tongue at just the right time, and I was grateful I had "treasured [it] in my heart" (Psalm 119:11).

When our children were young, Dave and I took a piece of cardboard, folded it in half and wrote a Scripture on each side. We kept it on the dining room table so that at our evening meals we could read it together and memorize it. We changed the Scripture each week. This simple tradition afforded us an opportunity to talk with our children about the meaning of the Word and its importance in our lives.

We can study God's Word on our own as we sit at His feet in private. The Bible is a Book to be read and understood, and with many good translations available today, we are without excuse. In addition, hundreds of books have been written to help us learn how to study with integrity and accurate interpretation. Your pastor or a leader in your church may be able to point you to one that would suit your spiritual maturity and needs.

Bible study in the fellowship of others who love Jesus can also help us sit at His feet. It can be a sweet, enriching experience to share His love letter to us, the Bible, with other Christians, and to exchange the insights we receive from the Holy Spirit. Women often benefit from Bible studies specifically designed for women, suited to women's particular needs. If there is none in your area, why not start one in your home? Get a couple of other women and study together one of the many Bible study books on the market.

Regardless of how we do it, studying God's Word is essential to understanding our Lover and knowing how to please Him.

2. Meditation

Meditation in its true Christian sense means reflecting on, pondering and contemplating God and His Word. We have lost this art, and in many cases have become suspicious of it, because the concept has been stolen by Eastern religions. But the practice of meditation still belongs to Christians, and we only cheat ourselves when we forsake it.

In his book *Keeping the Doors Open* (Chosen, 1992), author Peter Lord suggests that meditating on Scripture is different from Bible study in that we study with our left— or reasoning, figuring and information-storing—side of the brain. We meditate, however, with the right side, in which originate our more creative and imaginative faculties. Meditation, says Lord, involves opening our minds to the Holy Spirit, so He can

> call up information from the left side of our brains and . . . communicate through the right side as well. He may bring to mind a certain fact or point out false information and then renew our minds with right and true information. He may inspire our imaginations to picture different Bible characters in recorded incidents, and help us apply that understanding to our own situations. And He may give us His intuition to discern the correctness of motives and actions, our own and those of the people around us.

In meditation we think about our Lover, dwell on His goodness, realize His deity and accept His willingness to be with us in communion and not let go, regardless of how we are pulled away. It takes time to center your thoughts on the Lord and keep your mind stayed on Him. We may have to neglect some good things for this better thing, staying at His feet until our fellowship with Him is complete.

3. Prayer

If we want God's Spirit to overflow us, we must become women of prayer. In prayer the Holy Spirit fuses our union and shapes it into oneness. Prayer then becomes more than a ritual; it becomes the very breath of life that sustains us and changes our attitudes, desires and perceptions.

As we persist in knowing our Lover through prayer, we dare draw near to God in a way we never thought possible. We pray in order to know the heart and mind of our Lover, and His purposes for us and for the world. In his book *Prayer, a Holy Occupation* (Discovery House/Thomas Nelson, 1992), Oswald Chambers notes that

> the secret place [of prayer] convinces us that He is our Father, and that He is righteousness and love, and we remain not only unshaken but we receive our reward with an intimacy that is unspeakable and full of glory.

Imagine an intimacy with Jesus that is full of glory! You can have it in prayer.

Prayer, like praise, is an attitude. In 1 Thessalonians 5:17 Paul tells us to "pray without ceasing." This means nurturing intimacy throughout the day and night, maintaining an ongoing dialogue, a secret union in which the burdens of life cannot touch you. Gradually our Lover becomes our first thought on arising in the morning and our last thought as we close the day and commit ourselves into His care.

When you pray, always allow the Holy Spirit access. It is He who continues to whisper the love of Jesus deep within your soul. It is He who raises you to life and gives you power. In fact, it is through the Holy Spirit that your aching place is ultimately healed.

The key to our aching place lies within our spirit. When you and I received Jesus as Savior and Lord, we gave Him access to that key. The more intimate our relationship with

Him, the more able He is to unlock all our secret wounds and pour out His healing balm. He will bathe our aching places with the oil of His healing until we are finally one with Him and immersed in His full redemption. This healing flow from the Holy Spirit is renewed each time we pray.

Journaling is a marvelous way to keep your prayer life alive and vital. Some women are frightened by this suggestion, feeling it will be too demanding or time-consuming. Even writing a line or two each day, however, will be a blessing. Put down your feelings as you draw near to your Lover through prayer and reading His Word. Never be afraid to say what is in your heart. Not only will it cement your thoughts; it will also be a means by which you can look back and see all that God has done in your life.

It helps some women to have a prayer partner, someone with whom to share concerns and prayer in person or on the telephone. This should never take the place of personal, intimate conversation with Jesus, but it may help to boost your confidence and skills in praying.

4. Combining Your Prayer Life with the Word

When I first received Jesus into my heart, I discovered that I loved the Scriptures. So I began praying back to the Lord what they said. I wanted above all, for example, to be led by my Lover and to acknowledge Him in my life. So when I found Proverbs 3:5–6, I started praying it to Him daily.

"Lord," I would say, "I am trusting You with all my heart today. I dare not trust myself or try to stand in my own understanding. It might fail me. I acknowledge You in every way today, and I want to thank You for leading me. I know I can trust You." Then I might think about any areas in which it was hard for me to trust the Lord.

Long after this became my discipline, I learned that other Christians were doing the same thing. There are even books out now to help direct this kind of Word-prayer. But I encourage you to develop a system of your own. One way to do this is to divide a notebook into categories that concern you. (The number of categories will grow as time passes.)

Suppose, for instance, that one of your concerns is your low self-esteem. You need to strengthen your knowledge that you are important to your Lover. So begin praying back to Jesus what you now know He thinks of You, like this:

"I thank You, Jesus, that I am a child of God!" (Romans 8:16)

"I am grateful, Lord, that I am in Christ Jesus. You are my Savior, and even though I blow it sometimes, I have Your righteousness because of Your death and resurrection for me. When the devil whispers in my ear today, 'You've blown it big time,' I will answer that I am forgiven and have Your righteousness." (1 Corinthians 1:30)

"Lord, I am humbled by the fact that my life is no accident. You knit me in my mother's womb and know all about me. I can't even count how many times a day your thoughts turn toward me. You have created me and You knew me before I was ever born. I can never be lost to Your Spirit, and this makes me feel very special." (Psalm 139)

"Thank You, Jesus, that I am never condemned by You. Never! Sometimes I wonder why You love me so much, but I realize You will never stop, no matter how I push You away or fail You. I am not condemned, on account of Your mercy and grace." (Romans 8:1)

"I am more than a conqueror because of You, Jesus. You are my wonderful Lover, and I need to be reminded in the situation I am going through that You have already won the victory for me. I will always triumph in You and I thank You!" (Romans 8:37)

These are just a few of the Scriptures that can build your self-esteem in the Lord.

One rainy day I left my doctor's office with the news that I had a malignant tumor growing under my right eye. The doctor told me he had caught it early and that it was not life-threatening at this time. He informed me of the danger of radiation, because the tumor was so close to my eye, set a date for my surgery and told me we would discuss follow-up treatment in detail later.

As I got into my car, I felt overwhelmed. I wondered how this cancer would affect my future, my life span and my family. But because of the cancer's location, and because my doctor had indicated it was not life-threatening, I was more concerned about how much scarring would show on my face.

All the way home I thought about the scarring, but felt at peace. I knew the Lord was able to take care of me in all things. I decided the scars would be a constant reminder of God's grace in this early detection and would give me an opportunity to witness. I would be able to tell people firsthand how important it is to leave our outside appearance to Him.

That evening I went to my Bible and notebook to pray some Scriptures. I looked through all my categories, but nothing quite seemed to fit my situation. I thanked the Lord that His grace was sufficient for me, according to 2 Corinthians 12:9. I also thanked Him, according to Philippians 4:13, that I could do all things through Christ who gives me strength.

Then I turned to the Psalms and read these words:

> Why are you in despair, O my soul? And why have you become disturbed within me? Hope in God, for I shall yet praise Him, *the help of my countenance,* and my God.
> Psalm 42:11 (italics mine)

Jesus is the help of my countenance! I thought. I felt such a blessing of peace.

"Thank You, Jesus," I prayed, "that You are the help of my countenance. I don't have to worry about this cancer and its effects on my face because You are the light of my life. All I really want is for people to see You shining out of me."

I wrote the prayer in my book and released the operation to Jesus.

After surgery I learned an amazing thing. When the doctor cut into my face, he told me later, he found the cancer enclosed in a capsule-like "container." He plucked it from under my eye and stitched me up.

Naturally I looked pretty awful at first, with lots of stitching and bruising, but there was good news: The doctor did not feel I would need follow-up radiation. He was convinced he had removed all the cancer. I was pleased and went home to heal, still praying Psalm 42:11.

When it was time to have the stitches removed, I was awestruck at the results! I do have some scarring, but nothing like it could have been. People find it hard to believe such extensive surgery was done on my face.

How grateful I was! God had done for me far more than I ever dreamed. I went back to the Scripture the Lord had given me and prayed, "Lord, You are the help of my countenance, and how I praise You!" At that moment I felt the arms of my Lover close tightly around me. I would have been content to live with worse scars, but my Lover took care of them. Love rushed from my spirit to His heart of love.

You are God's cherished daughter, and all His promises of love belong to you. Search His Word for promises about all the issues that affect your life every day: fear, temptation, healing, the salvation of others and so on. Let Him speak to you tenderly as you pray His words back to Him. Your Lover will delight in your efforts.

5. Regular Evaluations of Your Walk with Jesus

Evaluate your relationship with Jesus regularly. Allow the Holy Spirit to shine His searchlight deep inside your spirit. The deeper He goes, the more He can detect. Let Him point out attitudes that need to go, little sins you have learned to tolerate, and let Him bring gently to your realization your need to be released from bondage.

Even as our Lover heals our past woundedness, He reminds us that He does not want us to remain introspective forever. Moving forward is part of His cure and plan so we do not become narcissistic in our inward looking. He can keep us from becoming bogged down, immobile in the process of healing.

The more we get to know Jesus through Bible study, meditation, prayer and Word-prayers, the more easily we will recognize His voice. In John 10 He said, "My sheep hear My voice" (verse 27). His voice is never condemning, never punitive. When we need correction, He offers it in a loving way that will not destroy us but lead us to repentance, cleansing and restoration.

In fact, it is a tremendous compliment when we find that our relationship with our Lover has grown to the place where He can point out things we really need to hear. He knows our spirits are tender and that we are prone to self-condemnation. He does not want to crush our sensitive spirits, but as we mature in His love, He can deal with us on a deeper level.

My friend Karen is very much in love with Jesus, and her walk with Him has become more and more intimate and fulfilling. She senses His deep abiding in her spirit as she follows His way, and she knows beyond a doubt that He cherishes her.

"One day," Karen recalls, "a peculiar cyst began to grow on my shoulder. I had no idea what it was, so I did nothing for several weeks, until it began to emit a foul odor."

So Karen called to ask her doctor to look at the cyst. While she waited for the day of her appointment to arrive, the cyst grew larger and the odor more vile. More concerned than ever, Karen began to pray.

"I want Your healing, Lord," she said.

But Jesus seemed silent as she entreated Him. Finally she cried out, "Help me understand Your silence."

With great love and tenderness He took her in His arms.

Karen, My daughter, He whispered to her spirit, *this cyst and its odor are like the hidden aroma of your spirit. It is offensive and must be cut out.*

Startled, Karen remembered some attitudes and subtle sins that were hard for her to release. She had kept them on a back burner and continued her intimacy with her Lover as though they were not there.

"How did you handle this revelation?" I asked when she told me her story. Many women, I knew, would have been unable to bear such strong correction.

"I fell on my knees before Jesus," she answered, "and asked Him to cut it out of me, as surely as the doctor was going to cut out the cyst. Jesus is aware of all that's in my heart and spirit, and those attitudes and sins were a stench to the One I love most of all! I asked His forgiveness and felt the refreshing of His cleansing."

Jesus knew Karen trusted Him enough and was secure enough in His love to hear such a deep correction. He dared, therefore, to point out something she might otherwise not have been able to receive. Her close union with Him gave Him freedom to deal with her honestly. Karen had shown maturity and a disciplined life in the Spirit.

What about you? Do you know His voice? Do you trust your Lover enough to submit to the evaluation of His Holy Spirit?

Be Creative in Loving Your Lover

The five disciplines listed above will please your Lover if you engage in them for the purpose of knowing and delighting in Him. Let me say it again: Incorporating them into your life will take time and effort. But these are part of the gift of yourself to Jesus.

Now, think for a moment about special gifts you have received from spouses, children, parents or friends. The time and effort that went into the choosing, purchasing and wrapping of those gifts meant a lot to you. But what other element made you feel loved, as if the giver had no one else in the world to think about but you?

Creativity. Anyone can buy a bottle of perfume. But when the perfume turns out to be a favorite you have craved for months, and it is wrapped in your signature color, you know the giver put special thought into pleasing you.

So add creativity to your time with Jesus. Here are some suggestions:

1. Spend ten minutes in verbal praise of your Lover.
2. Listen to a praise and worship tape, then turn it off and compose your own hymn of praise.
3. Write out a prayer of love to Jesus, taking time to choose your words carefully. Put it away for future use.
4. Close your eyes and take time to feel your Lover's arms around you as you express your love to Him.
5. Laugh out loud, and as you do, visualize Jesus laughing with you.
6. Fast one day and use the extra time in thanksgiving and praise for all Jesus means to you.
7. Call a lonely person and share a Scripture of encouragement.
8. Go to the hospital and volunteer to rock a newborn baby, praying for the blessing of Jesus in his or her life.

9. Read a good Christian book, then share it with someone.

10. Ask God to put someone "in your basket" to whom you can minister on a regular basis. Listen to him or her, and ask Jesus for an opportunity to share His love with this person.

Your Lover will delight in you and in every way you choose to draw near to Him. With disciplined time, effort and creativity, your love for Him will reach new heights. Even as He bathes your aching place with His tender affection and intervention, you will be ministering to Him.

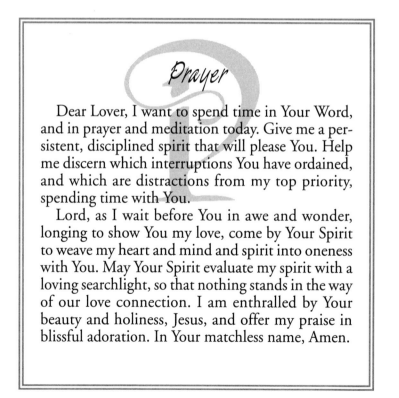

Prayer

Dear Lover, I want to spend time in Your Word, and in prayer and meditation today. Give me a persistent, disciplined spirit that will please You. Help me discern which interruptions You have ordained, and which are distractions from my top priority, spending time with You.

Lord, as I wait before You in awe and wonder, longing to show You my love, come by Your Spirit to weave my heart and mind and spirit into oneness with You. May Your Spirit evaluate my spirit with a loving searchlight, so that nothing stands in the way of our love connection. I am enthralled by Your beauty and holiness, Jesus, and offer my praise in blissful adoration. In Your matchless name, Amen.

13

Have You Entered In?

Many women have come to know Jesus as the Lover they need most. He longs to have this relationship with each of us, for it is in such intimacy that our aching places will find healing. And it is in such intimacy that our Lover will know the joy of fellowship with the beloved created ones for whom He died.

Have you entered the love connection with Jesus? Believing and accepting by faith His death on the cross for your salvation and His gift of eternal life are only the beginning of your journey. Many women believe this is all they need. But Jesus wants much more for you! The apostle Paul said we are also to "*know* Him, and the power of His resurrection" (Philippians 3:10, italics mine).

Knowing Jesus personally and in power will change not only our concepts of ourselves, but our understanding of life and other people as well.

How Do We Enter In?

The following three steps will help us understand how to enter in.

1. We Must Come

The prostitute we talked about in chapter 1 had heard Jesus speak. She could have left it at that. But in Luke 7 we read that she *came* to Jesus, fell at His feet and lavished on Him her love.

The Greek word for *come* in this passage is *sumpatheo,* which means "to be touched with feeling." The root word is *sumpathes,* which means "to have a similar feeling," and from it we get our word *sympathy.* That day the woman realized Jesus had sympathy for her! This wonderful vision of Jesus helped her grasp the enormity of His love and forgiveness, and gave birth in her life to spiritual intimacy.

Coming is where we always begin.

2. We Must Touch Jesus

The woman in Matthew 9 who had been bleeding for many years touched the hem of Jesus' garment. Why did she not simply brush against Him, touching His sleeve or shoulder?

This woman knew exactly what she was doing! All Jewish men wore a prayer shawl called a *tillet,* adorned at the hem with tassels or fringes call *ztit ztit.* The reason for these tassels is explained in Numbers 15:38–40, in which God told Moses:

> "Speak to the sons of Israel, and tell them that they shall make for themselves tassels on the corners of their garments throughout their generations, and that they shall put on the tassel of each corner a cord of blue. And it shall be a tassel for you to look at and remember all the commandments of the LORD, so as to do them and not follow after your own heart and your own eyes. . . ."

God was telling His male Jewish subjects that the tassels were to represent a constant reminder of His law, and their relationship to it and to Him.

So the woman with the hemorrhage was asking Jesus to "remember" her with sympathy. She believed Jesus would understand why she was touching His hem. And she had the confidence to say, "If I only touch His garment, I shall get well" (Matthew 9:21).

The word *whole* in this passage also has a rich, full meaning in the Greek. It is *sozo,* meaning "saved, delivered, protected." When Jesus touched this woman, she was totally delivered. In the fullest context of the Greek, this meant much more than physical healing. Her life was changed forever by this touch—and ours will be, too.

How do we touch Jesus? By telling Him our story and allowing His Holy Spirit to have control of our lives, as I described in chapters 2 and 3. We touch His heart as the Spirit overflows in us, causing us to know Him in His fullness. It is in coming and in touching that we are saved, delivered and protected.

But there is still one more step.

3. We Must Allow Jesus to Turn and Acknowledge Us

Mark's account of the story of the woman with the hemorrhage says that Jesus turned when He asked, "Who touched Me?" (Mark 5:31). The word *turned* here is from the root word *epi,* which means "to take charge of" or "to convert." When Jesus turned to acknowledge the woman, He was already causing conversion to take place; He was willing now to take charge of her life. As her fearful eyes met His loving, compassionate gaze, all the woundedness in her spirit was being washed away. In her heart she embraced the Lover of her life who could not only save and heal but take charge.

And why did Jesus acknowledge this woman? Why did He ask, "Who touched Me?" The disciples thought it was a foolish question to ask in the press of that surging crowd, but Jesus knew what He was doing. Mark 5:33 tells us that the woman trembled and fell at Jesus' feet, probably anticipating a reprimand from the Master.

Why do you suppose the ever-tender Jesus singled her out like this?

For the same reason He singles out you and me. He wants more than a passing acquaintance with us. He wants more than to offer us salvation and then go on His way. He wants intimacy with us. He wants to be our Lover.

Coming to Jesus, touching Him and allowing Him to turn and acknowledge us make all the difference in the world between *knowing of* our Lover, and *knowing Him,* and the power of His resurrection.

When You Fall in Love . . .

If you have ever fallen in love, or watched someone else fall in love, you know the byproducts are usually obvious. The beloved has a new spring in her step. Even the most familiar things in her life look new and wonderful to her. She feels beautiful, and her new self-confidence and joy overflow in kindness to those around her.

When we fall in love with Jesus, the results are obvious, too. When we are at peace within ourselves, and our aching place is being bathed in healing every day, we are more enjoyable to be around. We can accept correction without feeling condemned or defensive. We become vulnerable to others and accept, love and forgive them as Jesus does us, because they are not our sources of identity or self-esteem.

Sitting at the feet of Jesus daily, submitting to Him and walking in His Spirit will free His healing stream to soothe our hurts and free us from bondage. We in turn will begin to blossom under His care.

Have you entered in? Your Lover knows every facet of your being—past, present and future—yet loves you uncon-ditionally. He will touch you in ways no one else can. He wants to become the joy and delight of your life. Accord-ing to Zephaniah 3:17, ". . . He will exult over you with joy, He will be quiet in His love, He will rejoice over you with shouts of joy."

You can spend a lifetime trying to win His approval, when in reality you already have it. You can try to serve Him with your whole heart, yet miss the pleasure He takes in you as His daughter.

Do not let doubt, fear, past wounds or present circumstances keep you from this life-giving, Spirit-filled relationship. Commit to making Jesus the Lover you have always needed most, the Healer of your aching place.

He stands ready. Embrace Him!

Prayer

O Jesus, the Lover and joy of my life, a wealth of love and intimacy is available to me in my relationship with You. Touch me, Lord, as I come to You by faith. Free me from all hindrances as You turn toward me. Give me passion for Your precious Word and zeal in prayer. Arrange all my priorities so that nothing is of higher value than sitting at Your feet to know You completely. Make our mutual love the vital, freeing force of my life.

I stand in awe of You, Jesus. I will always be amazed and thrilled with Your grace and the fact that You delight in me. I feel the warmth of Your healing as You bathe me in Your Spirit. You are all I will ever need. Keep me winsomely one with You forever! Amen.

Jan McCray is a Bible teacher and seminar and retreat leader throughout the U.S. and abroad. The goal of her ministry: to evangelize and strengthen the Body of Christ through preaching, teaching and personal follow-up. Jan has also served several times as a short-term missionary to Kenya working among the Maasai. The mother of three and grandmother of four, she has a master's degree in Judaic studies and lives with her husband, David, in St. Petersburg, Florida.

Jan is available to speak or teach. More information about her ministry can be secured by writing:

Jan McCray Ministries, Inc.
P.O. Box 47176
St. Petersburg, FL 33743